Buy Right, Sell High

Robert Irwin

**Real Estate
Education Company®**
a division of Dearborn Financial Publishing, Inc.

This publication is designed to provide accurate and authoritative information in regard to the subject matter covered. It is sold with the understanding that the publisher is not engaged in rendering legal, accounting, or other professional service. If legal advice or other expert assistance is required, the services of a competent professional person should be sought.

Executive Editor: Cynthia A. Zigmund
Managing Editor: Jack Kiburz
Interior Design: Lucy Jenkins
Cover Design: S. Laird Jenkins Corporation

Published by Real Estate Education Company®,
a division of Dearborn Financial Publishing, Inc.®

Printed in the United States of America

97 98 99   10 9 8 7 6 5 4 3 2 1

Library of Congress Cataloging-in-Publication Data

Irwin, Robert, 1941–
    Buy right, sell high / Robert Irwin.
        p.   cm.
    Includes index.
    ISBN 0-7931-2445-X (pbk.)
        1. House buying–United States.   2. House selling–United States.
    I. Title.
    HD1379.I6417   1997
    643′.12–dc21   97-2316
                                                            CIP

Real Estate Education Company books are available at special quantity discounts to use as premiums and sales promotions, or for use in corporate training programs. For more information, please call the Special Sales Manager at 800-621-9621, ext. 4384, or write to Dearborn Financial Publishing, Inc., 155 N. Wacker Drive, Chicago, IL 60606-1719.

BOOKS BY ROBERT IRWIN

Buy Your First Home!

Find It, Buy It, Fix It: The Insider's Guide to Fixer-Uppers

For Sale by Owner Kit

Home Inspection Troubleshooter

Home Remodeling Organizer

Landlord's Troubleshooter

CONTENTS

PREFACE

There was a time when you could just throw money at real estate, have it stick, and know it would come back as profit.

Not any more.

If there's one thing that the great real estate recession of the early 1990s proved, it was that home prices could go down just as well as they could go up. While the market has turned around in most areas, we all know it could just as easily turn down again. This means that today if you're considering the purchase of a home, whether it be a single-family dwelling, a condo, townhouse, or co-op, you must carefully consider your future resale possibilities. Will you be able to resell today's investment for a profit? Will you be able to break even? Will it be a loss? (If it's going to be a loss, maybe you'd be better off not buying at all.)

These are not the sort of considerations that the average homebuyer is used to making. Rather, most of us tend to spend our efforts in finding a house that will fit us best: Is it the right size? Do we like the layout? Does it have a big enough garage? Is there room for our piano? Is it close to shopping and schools?

Indeed, virtually all of the many books on buying real estate simply address finding the home that will best suit your needs and wants. If they even consider future resale possibilities, it is usually only briefly.

Today, the serious money required demands that you look at the purchase of a home with a highly critical eye. When you spend $100,000, $200,000, $300,000, or more, you can't afford to just hope that things will all work out in the end. You need some assurance that you're making a wise purchase.

Buy Right, Sell High is the one book that guides you through the reselling considerations you need to make at the time you buy your next home. It is devoted entirely to getting you a profit (or at the least breaking even) when you resell. Yes, I'll talk about getting the house of your dreams. But, at every turn I'll ask if the purchase you're considering right now makes good investment sense for the future. The minimum goal of this book is to keep you from losing money on your real estate purchase. The maximum goal is to see that you make lots of money on the deal.

I'll discuss how to be a "ruthless" buyer, so that you get a deal that's good for you, and how to look at a house with investor's eyes (Chapters 1 to 3). In addition to location (Chapter 4), I'll look at design (Chapter 5), size (Chapter 7), buying new or old (Chapter 8), and possible environmental problems with the property (Chapter 6). You'll also learn how to plan for resale by evaluating the market and leaving a back door open (Chapters 9 through 12) and take a look at tax planning (Chapter 15) as well as special concerns with condos and co-ops (Chapter 14).

In short, *Buy Right, Sell High* is your complete guide to buying a profitable home. Use it well and you won't have to worry that your dream house could become a financial nightmare.

CHAPTER 1

Don't Buy Wrong

This is actually a book about selling your *next* home. Yet, it doesn't have anything to do with selling or the sale itself. Rather, everything you will find in this book has to do with buying and preparing you to buy–correctly.

The premise is simple. If you buy correctly, then you will have no trouble later on selling quickly and for a profit–buy right, sell high!

Sounds easy, doesn't it? But does it really work like that?

In fact, it does. If you purchase the right home in the right location, for the right price with the right terms, you'll have no trouble reselling–in any market. On the other hand, if you buy wrong, you'll end up selling low no matter how good the market.

Many people experienced the downside of this fact in very real terms during the great real estate recession of the early 1990s. Before this recent market downturn, however, few people were aware of it. In fact, up until about 1989 it was very hard to lose in real estate. If you bought right, you made a very sweet profit. If you bought wrong, well, the worst that was likely to happen was that you made a few less bucks in profit. In other words, the penalty in the past for buying wrong was not very great.

Not so anymore. Millions of homeowners personally experienced what can happen when you buy wrong during the recent real estate recession. When the market turned sour, those who had not bought well often could barely get out breaking even. A great many were forced to sell at a substantial loss. And many individuals simply couldn't sell at all, often losing their homes to foreclosure. In a bad market, buying wrong is like the kiss of death. You end up with a moribund property that nobody wants, including yourself.

But can you buy right? Is it possible for the average homebuyer to anticipate and plan ahead so that no matter what happens in the market, no matter what other factors might come along, you are able to resell successfully?

Actually, it is possible to protect yourself from a down market and maximize your profits in an up market. We'll see how to do just that in the next chapters. But to begin, let's talk about perspective. What's your homebuying perspective?

Are You a Consumer of Real Estate?

Economists are fond of pointing out that we are a nation of consumers. Most of the time we just buy things to use them up. We are, so to speak, at the bottom of the food chain when it comes to products.

Consider a refrigerator. My wife and I recently needed one, so we went to various stores to consider our options, which were plentiful. There were refrigerators with glass shelves, with ice and water dispensers, and with vertical or horizontal storage spaces. Prices ranged from a low of around $300 for the stripped-down model to close to $2,000 for the superdeluxe version, loaded with everything, except, of course, food.

Salespeople plied us with arguments why this brand was better than the other one. Some refrigerator models had a special low level of operation that would cut down our costs in summer. Others offered an optional "humid" mode that could handle hot, wet weather better. Yet others were "space savers" that somehow managed to fit more cubic feet into a smaller area. (The salesperson didn't come right out and say so but implied these were somehow bigger on the inside than on the outside!)

Yet through all of the options, the models, the manufacturers, and the arguments about which was better, never once did any salesperson (or indeed did we) ask, "How much profit will I make when I resell this refrigerator?"

If that's a surprising question, ask yourself, "Why should it be?" Is it so unreasonable to expect that if you pop for a $1,000 item today, it should be worth $1,100 tomorrow?

The Consumer Food Chain

Apparently so, when it comes to refrigerators. As I said, we're at the bottom of the food chain, here. The companies that produce the metal, the ceramics and plastic, the glass, and the motor and the compressor that go into the refrigerator all make a profit. The company that assembles the refrigerator and puts its label on it makes a profit. The wholesaler/distributor tacks on a profit. And, finally, the retailer who sells it to us makes his or her profit, too.

But what about us? We just pay! We pay for the profits the others make!

The minute my wife and I had that big refrigerator wheeled out of the store, it was worth at least 25 percent to 30 percent less, assuming we could even get someone to buy it. And finding a buyer isn't easy. I have a friend who owns an apartment complex that doesn't supply refrigerators to tenants. New tenants are constantly buying refrigerators when they move in, and then when they leave, trying to sell them. The trouble is that few people want even a slightly used refrigerator, unless they can get it at a bargain price. Typically, the tenants pay upward of $500 for the refrigerator and then try to resell it for $250 a few months later. Many accept less just to avoid having to pay the costs of moving it.

It's even worse for those of us who keep that refrigerator for a reasonable period of time, say five years. If we then decide to buy a new one, we'd be lucky to get a hundred bucks for the old unit—an item that we may have paid well over a thousand dollars for originally.

In short, we *consume* refrigerators. We are like the last fish on the food chain. We give everyone else a profit, except ourselves. And what is undoubtedly the worst about this, we don't give any of it a second thought—we just assume that's the way things are supposed to be!

In our culture, in fact, that's the way things are with most items from refrigerators to cars, from furniture to television sets, from clothing to jewelry. We buy virtually everything to *use* it up; we think of our purchases in terms of consuming. And this is what gets us into trouble when it comes time to buy our home.

The Biggest Consumable Item?

For most people, buying a home is *the* single biggest purchase made in a lifetime. Not too many of us are out there buying other items that cost $100,000, $200,000, $300,000, or more. A home is the ultimate big purchase. Yet, we usually come to the home purchase not with the detachment of an investor, but with the hungry eyes of a consumer.

For almost our entire lives we have been trained to consume, and most of us are pretty darned good at it. (I have a friend who swears that his wife has a black belt in mall shopping!) When we look at a home we are thinking about buying, we use all of the many consumer's tricks at our disposal.

Is it the right color? Will our furniture fit in or will we have to buy new couches, beds and so on? Is it going to be big enough for ourselves and for our child(ren)? Does it have a large enough garage to accommodate all our cars? Are the living and family rooms spacious enough for us to stretch out and feel comfortable in? Will we need to put in new carpeting or otherwise spend more on redecorating the place to our liking?

What about the kitchen? Is it "our size"? Is it big enough to handle all the appliances we own (have consumed), with enough counterspace to work on?

What about the bathrooms? Are there lots of them? (We Americans like plentiful, big bathrooms—in Europe, people aren't so interested in the bathroom, but instead they devote more time to the size and comfort of the bedrooms.)

What about the grounds? Is everything landscaped? Is the lawn green and the shrubbery well trimmed?

And what about the neighbors? Is the neighborhood pleasant, well kept, and quiet? Do the neighbors have cars of approximately the same quality as our own? (You'd be astonished how many buyers, in their hearts, judge a neighborhood by whether the cars in the driveways are newer or older, well kept or falling apart, Fords, GMs, and Chryslers or BMWs, Mercedes, and Lexuses.)

If we take a moment to be scrupulously honest, most of us have to admit that we spend at least a little time "keeping up with the Joneses" and that applies particularly to the neighborhood. Most of us want to live in an area that we can be proud of and, just maybe, show off a little bit. And why not? After all, presumably we work hard for our living, so why not reap the rewards of living in a better neighborhood? Given the choice, wouldn't you opt for a more prestigious neighborhood than the one in which you now live? If you think not, then ask yourself, would you opt for a less prestigious neighborhood?

In short, when we consider the purchase of a home, most of us look with a consumer's eyes. We've been trained to. We behave like the last fish in the food chain. All our lives we've been buying things to use up and throw away. It's what comes natural to us living in this century, in this country. And during our lifetime of consumerism, most of us have honed our purchasing abilities to a fine sharpness so that we can spy out just what we will like and snag it.

Is What We Like What We Should Buy?

But there's the dilemma: What if the house we really like, the one that our consumer's eyes tell us is just perfect for our need and wants, isn't the right one? By that I mean, what if buying it is a mistake, in terms of our ability to resell later on at a profit?

Most people don't really consider reselling at the time they buy, even though that should be the paramount question. Oh, we might take a moment to ponder whether or not the place will be easy or hard to resell, but then most people just assume that thinking that far ahead is unproductive. Besides, we think, most things will take care of themselves in the future.

I've gone out with a great many buyers during my lifetime and very few of them ever gave serious consideration, at the time they bought, to reselling. There are exceptions, of course, particularly in the case of those whose jobs require them to move frequently. These movers realize they're going to be in a house for a very short time, only six months or a year or two or whatever, and they are indeed concerned about reselling.

But that's not the case for most people. Most of us just see the house as another consumable item. We want to make it ours, to use up for our satisfaction, to enjoy to the fullest. We're concerned with the here and now, not with the uncertainty of the future.

How Long Will You Live There?

But the future will arrive and you will, statistically speaking, try to resell the house you are buying and, in all likelihood, in not so many years from now as you may believe. According to government statistics, the average family sells its home every seven to nine years. That's not such a very long time.

Yet my experience has been that most people tend to overlook the possibility of a resale only a few years down the road. They refuse to seriously consider it at the time they buy. In short, with the rare exception of those who know up front that a job is going to require a move in the very near future, most of us don't really anticipate ever reselling.

Oh, we know that it could happen. But deep down at some primitive level, we ignore the possibility and we buy for eternity.

If you don't think you're in this group, the next time you consider the purchase of a home (presumably this is going to be soon now, because you're reading this book), ask yourself, "*Exactly* how long will I live here?"

Put a number to it. Is this going to be your home for one year? Three years? Ten years? Twenty? Forever?

If you answered more than five years, what you're actually saying is that in terms of anticipation, you're probably looking to move in and stay put as if you intended to live there forever. No, you might not come right out and say, "Forever," but the effect is the same.

Of course, from a psychological perspective this is nothing more than a healthy attitude. There's nothing wrong with acting as if you're going to live in a house forever. It is part and parcel of making a "house into a home." In some ways, you do have to feel like you're going to live there forever to take psychological ownership, to make it yours and not something temporary like a rented apartment.

On the other hand, it has very little to do with making a sound financial decision. While you may act as though you are going to live there forever, you're far better off if you plan as if you're going to have to move tomorrow.

Do You Have the Right Perspective?

The problem really comes down to one of *perception.* When we buy, most of us look at a home in terms of what it can do for us now. Will this home satisfy our needs as we live in it (consume it)? If it's not a good fit, we reject the property. If it is a good fit, we tend to buy it. In other words, we make the purchase as if it were any other kind of consumable product, just like a TV or a refrigerator.

Is it any wonder, then, that when it comes time to resell, we often "suddenly" discover that we don't have a very salable item? Because we never bought with an eye toward reselling, finding another buyer "suddenly" becomes tough. (In fact, some houses are just as hard to sell as are used refrigerators!)

But, we may argue, we love this place. Why won't someone else come in, love it just like we do, and pay us a profit when they buy it?

Simple. The chances are the next buyer is just like us, another consumer. And that buyer is looking for exactly what will fit his or her needs or wants. The trouble is that the chances are truly remote that what one buyer wants is exactly the same as what another buyer wants.

Letting Go of Consumerism

Buying a home involves too much money to leave reselling to chance. If you're like the rest of us, you want to make a profit not suffer a loss when you eventually dispose of that wonderful house you're considering.

That being the case, the time to act decisively is now, not then when it's too late. (When it's time to sell you can wish you had bought a different house, but you're stuck with the one you did buy.)

So what do you do? Simple, at least in concept: instead of buying a house as if it were a refrigerator, buy a house as if it were a stock, a bond, or a commodity—in other words, an investment. We'll have more to say about your "home investment" in the next chapter.

*H*ome Buying Consumer Checklist

Have you checked:

- ❏ To see if the color is right?
- ❏ If your furniture will fit?
- ❏ If it's big enough for you, your spouse, and the kids?
- ❏ If it has a garage large enough for all your cars?
- ❏ If you can live with the carpeting?
- ❏ If the kitchen is suitable for your culinary needs?
- ❏ If the bathrooms are well decorated?
- ❏ If the landscaping is green and attractive?
- ❏ If the neighbor's cars are similar to yours?
- ❏ If the home will make your friends take notice?

The more items you checked, the bigger a consumer you are. If you checked them all, ask yourself if you've ever sold for a profit anything you've ever bought!

CHAPTER 2

Are You an Investor or a Consumer?

This is really a book about the two paths you can take when you buy your next house (or condo, town house or co-op). One path we'll call "consumption" (as described in the past chapter) and it can lead to lots of fun and pleasure while you're living in the house. But it can also mean financial disaster when it comes time to resell.

The other path we'll call "investing." Taking this trail may mean that you give up some of the comforts you might enjoy if you bought the house strictly as a consumer. But, in exchange, you'll be getting the ability to resell later on quickly and at a good price. In the past chapter we considered buying a house to keep up with the Joneses, to fit perfectly with your lifestyle and desires, and so on. In this chapter we're going to see how an *investor* picks out a property.

And then at the end of this chapter, we'll try to reconcile the two paths and have them blend into one so that you can get both the house you want and the house you should buy.

Do You Have an Investor's Approach?

In some ways it's easier for me to envision purchasing a home as an investor than as a consumer. That's probably because I've bought so many investment homes over the years.

What's an investment home? It's one that you buy strictly with an eye toward how easily and for how much it can be rented out now and for how quickly, how soon, and for how much profit it can be resold later. Like buying stocks, bonds, and commodities, it's purchasing a thing for its potential to return a profit. If you've never bought an investment home (or even if you have), you might find the following analysis refreshing, maybe even eye-opening.

Investing in Location

It's been said a great many times, but it's still worth repeating the three most important words influencing real estate investment are *location, location* and *location*. To an investor, finding the right location is like the search for the Holy Grail. The right location means profit. (Of course, there are other factors affecting profit, which we'll go into shortly.)

When buying an investment house, an investor may have the luxury of selecting a location from a wide area. Here is the breakdown that a wise investor will consider, from the most general to the most specific:

- State
- County
- City
- Neighborhood
- Street
- Exposure on the street

Of course, you probably won't have the latitude that an investor has. You're going to be living in the home, so the most restricting factor is more likely to be job location. Most of us want to be no more than an hour from work, if possible. (In truth, most investors are limited in a similar way—taking care of a rental usually means that they shouldn't be more than an hour's drive away from the property.)

Our likely choices are going to be within a certain county and within probably one or two cities. Now, however, the investor's path diverges significantly from that of the consumer.

An investor is going to view neighborhoods in a very dispassionate way. In fact, he or she doesn't really even have to see the neighborhood to make a choice. The investor doesn't care whether the house is colonial or ranch in design, whether it is on hilly or flat land, whether the area is filled with lovely old trees or has a very modern, stark appeal. What the investor wants to know is resale values. How much have houses in the neighborhood appreciated in the past and how much are they likely to appreciate in the future?

Surprisingly, much of this kind of information is available from most real estate agents. Today almost all are connected by modem to a central database where they can search for sales by neighborhood, going back six months to a year. Many can go back five years. That's the most helpful. What an investor wants to know is what the average price appreciation is year by year. Is it 5 percent? If so, the neighborhood's red hot. Is it -2 percent? Don't buy there.

If it's a tract home (as the vast majority of houses are), a data search can even tell which model has appreciated the fastest, by sales records. The computer program searching sales also can often tell what the best size of a home is, in terms of resale, as well as the optimum number of bedrooms and baths.

In other words, the investor doesn't pick neighborhoods by driving down streets and looking to see which are most appealing. Rather, the investor picks them from statistical facts. Even if the investor is brand new in a town, by the time he or she leaves an agent's office, the investor has a couple of prime neighborhoods in mind, knows the top models, and understands the minimum parameters in terms of bedrooms, baths, and the overall size of the home. (How does that compare with the way you shopped for your last house?)

We'll have much more to say about location in a later chapter, but for now, it is sufficient to point out that the investor's approach is methodical and by the books. What's important to notice is that personal preference plays no part in it. Never, never does the investor ask, "Do I *like* this type of house?" or "Will I feel comfortable in this neighborhood?" These questions are irrelevant . . . to the investor.

Old versus Brand New?

Most of the time, wise investors prefer houses that are at least five years old, because a track record of appreciation has been established and because most defects will have become apparent and will have been corrected by then. But sometimes, particularly in a hot market, investors will speculate with brand-new homes.

Perhaps a new industry has moved in bringing many new jobs with it. The new employees have quickly bought out the supply of existing homes and are literally waiting in line for more homes to come onto the market. The new home market is hot.

And it's here that investors will, sometimes, actually wait in line to purchase a brand-new home with the sole intention of holding it for a few months and then reselling it for a profit, once the rest of the new homes have been sold. In this situation, an investor/speculator will typically want the low- to middle-priced home in a development. The idea is that when the development is finished and prices begin to rise in a high-demand market, the lower-priced homes often will see the fastest appreciation. (The general rule is that the least expensive home in a neighborhood will get the fastest sale and the best price appreciation. This doesn't always hold true, but the odds do favor it.)

Note that the investor/speculator again doesn't care a whit about what the house looks like, what color it's painted, whether there's a wet bar in the family room or a separate shower and bath in the master bathroom. Other than to be sure the house is actually there, built and with no defects, the investor/speculator may not even check it over! The goal is simply to deal with the property as a commodity—something to be bought and resold, hopefully at a profit. (Again, how does this compare with the way you judged the purchase of your last home?)

How Much Money Can I Expect to Make?

Before actually making the purchase, however, investors will go over the numbers if not on paper at least in their heads. They want to know, basically, what their risk-to-return is. How much money do they have to put up in hopes of getting how big a profit?

The general rule for investors is to put as little of their money into the deal as possible to maximize the rewards. In other words, if they put $5,000 in and then resell for a profit of $10,000, they've made 200 percent on their money. If they put $50,000 in and resell for a profit of $10,000, they've only made 20 percent on their money. Two hundred percent is always better than 20 percent. A consumer, however, will often put down more money in order to make lower payments.

Many times investors will endure higher payments because they anticipate they'll only own the property for a short time and they'll be able to make up any loss from monthly payments by the profit when they sell.

The whole idea behind this is that there must be enough profit to be made on reselling to make the buying and the holding period worthwhile. As a result, investors often will anticipate inflation, the movement of the market (especially how hot it is), and how long it will take to resell at a profit. Only if the numbers make sense do investors act.

Note that the investor is not much concerned with the consumer question of whether or not the monthly payments are affordable over the long haul. The eye is always on reselling, as soon as possible, for a profit.

Furthermore, in a bad market, an investor may conclude that not only is there no profit to be made, but there is, in fact the likelihood of a loss if the house is purchased. Therefore, the investor may simply *pass* and not buy at all. The investor is not swayed by arguments such as the house is close by his or her work, the money to buy is saved and available, or the payments are finally affordable. The only math that matters is profit or loss.

How Do I Get Out If Things Go Bad?

Finally, the wise investor always leaves a back door out. What if the market crashes? It can and has happened. An industry suddenly leaves the area and jobs dry up. Suddenly everyone wants to sell their homes and the market plummets.

Or new developers pour into the area and build loads of new homes. This puts the skids on resales, and the market, which had been hot, flattens out.

Or something happens to the investor. Perhaps his or her personal financial fortunes wane. Or financing that the investor was anticipating doesn't develop. Or maybe even sickness hits and the investor can't care for the property as he or she had anticipated.

The wise investor always anticipates the unanticipated and provides a back door, a way to get out of the property if the worst happens, if the sky falls.

What kind of backdoor options does the wise investor have? We'll discuss these in detail in a later chapter, but for now, let's say that they often involve assumable mortgages, options with other investors or buyers, or some other creative device. In other words, if the market collapses, the wise investor *still* can get rid of the property.

Notice that the investor plans ahead both for profit and for the possibility of hard times *at the time of purchase.*

Consumer Path or Investor Path?

The two paths, consumer and investor, are as different as night and day. One is entirely personal, aiming to satisfy the needs and wants of the buyer. The other is entirely businesslike, aiming one-sightedly at the goal of making a profit.

Which path should you take?

It's probably safe to say that when it comes to buying a home, most of us have been on the consumer path for a long time. We use our heart when we buy most things, including our home. Only those who have actually dabbled in real estate investing have tried the other course. And frequently, even investors use one path for their for-profit purchase and another for their to-live-in purchases.

The premise of this book, however, is that to succeed in the modern real estate market, you must make sure these two separate paths actually cross. You must not be just a consumer of homes but an investor in homes as well. You must build the roads so that they run together, so that not only do you buy with your heart, but you buy with your head as well. Only then can you be safely assured of selling high, for a good profit.

The Fine Art of Compromise

How do you reconcile profit with pleasure, attune selling high with buying right?

I suggest fear and loathing. I've always felt that fear was a great motivator and I think it actually can help here, too. To see how, let's go back to the great tulip-bulb inflation in Denmark during the 20th century. At that time, the price of tulip bulbs, for whatever reason, suddenly began going up. This, coincidentally, happened to occur at the same time that they were offered for sale as financial investments on several markets.

Interest in tulip bulbs soared, and included people who had probably never given them a moment's thought before. Individuals poured money in, and prices rose higher and higher. Obviously, it was a fool's scheme. Eventually everyone realized that the bulbs were, after all, just flowers and the market crashed, with the last fool to buy losing everything.

Something similar happened to the real estate market at the end of the 1980s in most parts of the country. People began to think that real estate was, like the tulips before, a panacea to profit. Prices would only go higher and higher. So people bought and bought. In time, the market became untenable. Everyone realized that they were just dealing in houses, after all. Prices crashed.

The trouble was that the last fool into the game happened to be about 60 million Americans who had either bought at the peak of the market, had seen their home value skyrocket and had borrowed against that inflated equity, or just felt that their house was worth a lot more money than it really was.

When prices fell to more realistic levels, a great many people were disappointed. A whole lot more were financially hurt. And there were even a great many who lost their homes, their credit, and their savings.

A great, great many of these people now fear real estate. They don't want to buy for fear of losing.

But that makes no more sense that being afraid to smell tulips because the market crashed. Real estate remains an excellent investment. It's also a necessity—we all have to live someplace.

Therefore, if you have developed any fear at all of the real estate market (as evidenced by the fact that when you consider buying a home, you think back to what happened in the marketplace just a few years ago, wince, and worry if that could happen to you), I suggest you use that fear constructively. By that, I mean compromise a little bit when you buy.

Instead of buying a home simply as a consumable, also look at it as an investment. Instead of buying simply the most you can afford to satisfy your wants, become a bit more critical and purchase with the goal of reselling and making a profit.

This is not to say that you simply become an investor. Investors really don't care what they buy, as long as they can make a profit on it. But perhaps you can find something to buy that will not only be profitable, but that you will enjoy owning as well. You need to make the two different paths meet.

A New Perspective?

In fact, most people already do consider a real estate home purchase an investment, at least a little bit. We've always given a minimum amount of lip service to the idea that we're buying for profit as well as for comfort.

What I'm suggesting now, however, is that we walk much more on the investment path and much less on the consumable path. Instead of buying a home *mainly* to use it up and enjoy it, let's buy a home *primarily* to profit from it.

Thinking and acting this way has consequences. It probably means we won't get a house that we will like quite so well. But, it also means that we'll buy a place that we can sell later on at a higher price.

Remember, you don't have to be just a consumer. You have a choice. You can choose the path of gratification and get the house of your dreams. Or you can compromise a bit and choose the path that yields a profit, a house that won't turn into a nightmare.

---

*H*ome Buying Investor Checklist

Did you:

❑ Check to see if it's located in the best part of the county?

❑ Check to see if it's located in the best part of the city?

❑ Check to see if it's in the best part of the neighborhood?

❑ Check to see which areas have the fastest appreciation?

❑ Ask which home models sell quickest?

❑ Look for the least expensive house in a neighborhood?

❑ Figure out how to put in as little money as possible?

❑ Calculate the profit you anticipate making when you resell?

❑ Believe that prices won't always go up?

❑ Believe that prices won't always go down?

Lots of checks here suggests that you're an investor. Few checks indicate that you're still looking too much with your heart.

CHAPTER 3

Be a Ruthless Buyer

In 1986, a movie was released that starred Bette Midler called *Ruthless People.* In it two actors, Judge Reinhold and Helen Slater, became so financially desperate that they kidnapped a rich man's wife (Midler) and held her for ransom.

What made the movie so wonderful was that instead of being serious, it was a comedy. The rich man, played by Danny DeVito, wouldn't pay the ransom because he was happy to get rid of his wife. The kidnappers were really softhearted and sympathetic to Midler. She, in turn, was so outraged by her husband that she helped them collect the ransom! In the end, everyone went as their heart (not their heads) dictated and it was great fun for the audience.

Of course, it was just the movies. Real life usually isn't as kind . . . or as much fun.

However, there was an element of truth in the story that's well taken here; namely, nice people trying to act ruthless can benefit themselves. Inevitably, their hearts won out, as may be the case when we buy a home. Before that happened, they at least attempted to let their heads direct their actions.

Now I'm not suggesting that you kidnap anyone; in this chapter I am asking you to at least make the effort to be ruthless when you make a home purchase. Be ruthless toward the seller, toward the agent, and most of all, toward yourself.

Why Be Ruthless?

There are a lot of dictionary synonyms for ruthless including "inhuman," "atrocious," "barbaric," "vicious," "infamous," and "despicable." You can certainly be all these things if it helps you to get a better deal on a house. But they probably won't, and that's not what I'm suggesting here. Rather, by ruthless I mean that you aim to be determined, relentless, unstoppable in getting just what you want.

Why is this necessary? Why should a buyer be "ruthless"?

The answer is that when you buy with your eye toward investment, that is to say toward reselling, you're not going to get much help from anyone else. You may not even get much help from yourself! You're pretty much on your own.

As an aside, you might be your own worst enemy! For example, when you're a consumer, everyone along the way wants to help you. They want you to get the right color and the right layout. They want you to have just the right lawn and the cute little wet bar in the family room. And why not? After all, you're going to be giving them a profit and a commission. Even you, yourself, will be thrilled about selecting this or that because you'll be buying for you, letting your own whims and desires determine what you get. In fact, being a consumer is almost like taking a narcotic it's so personally pleasing. (Indeed, there are people who cannot help themselves and buy [consume] whenever they feel bad or depressed.)

Thus, the only way to really overcome our own self-aggrandizement, to "kick the consumption habit," so to speak, is to be ruthless about how we go about buying a house. If we aren't fully determined and relentlessly persevere in our goal of buying right, we'll simply slip onto the wrong path and very quickly find we are buying for our tastes, not for future resale.

To put it another way, when buying a home, it's very hard to see as an investor and very easy to feel like a consumer.

How Can I Be Ruthless with an Agent?

When most people begin house hunting, they contact an agent and the first thing out of their mouths is, "We're looking for a home to live in."

The agent, having loads of experience with people in exactly this situation, immediately begins honing in on your consumer needs: how many are in your family (how big a house do you need), is there any particular style you like (ranch, modern, Victorian, and so on), where do you work (where would you *like* to live), and so on?

By the time you've answered the agent's questions, you're a gone goose. You're deep into your own desires and the agent has neatly categorized you as a typical homebuyer. You'll see only properties that you find personally satisfying and except for such puffery as, "These homes really hold their value" or "You can't go wrong buying here," there'll be nary a word about resale and profit.

Do you see where this all went wrong? You got off course with the very first statement.

When you meet with an agent, don't say that you're looking for a home to live in. Instead say, "We're looking for investment property."

Instantly, a whole different set of parameters shift in the agent's mind. (You may, in fact, even be referred to a different agent who handles only investments!) No longer are you going to hear about room colors, layouts, and what kind of kitchen appliances you like. Now, it's going to be a different story.

The agent is going to begin by asking you what type of property you want to invest in: single-family, duplex, multiple-family, large apartment building, industrial, commercial. There's a long list.

You simply say you're looking for a single-family house (or condo or co-op). Nothing wrong with that. Millions of Americans invest in single-unit residential real estate all the time.

The next question the agent is going to ask, if he or she is any good, is something regarding the structure of the investment you have in mind. For example, "How long do you intend holding the property before you resell?" Or, "We have some nice properties, but they'll bring in a negative cash flow. Can you handle some negative?"

What the agent is really asking is what your timeline is and how strong a buyer you are.

How long you plan to hold a property is really asking whether you're looking for a property you can immediately turn around and resell for a profit, or if you're willing to wait a few years until inflation and a better market increases prices. (We'll have much more to say about this in a later chapter.) Asking about "negative" means that the rental income probably won't cover the monthly payments (principal, interest, taxes, insurance, maintenance, etc.). How much cash each month out of your pocket are you willing to put into the property to help make those payments?

Now you must ruthlessly keep to the investment path and answer something like, "I'd like to be able to resell soon, if necessary, but I'm willing to hold for a while. And we plan to live in the property, so we can handle monthly payments up to $X. (We'll see how to calculate how much you can afford to pay in a later chapter.)

At this point, the agent will undoubtedly draw back, give a big "Hmm?" and ask, "You're going to live in the property? So you want a home for yourself?"

If you aren't careful, this can be a critical juncture between the two paths. Say "Yes," and you're back on the consumer path. Everything from there on out will be geared toward your pleasure.

What you want to say is "No, I'm looking strictly for investment property. We only plan to live in it temporarily." ("Temporarily," of course, meaning until you resell!)

The agent may look at you strangely and think you're an unusual duck. But you have clearly defined your parameters. You're looking strictly for property that can be bought as an investment and that's what you expect the agent to show you.

How Can I Be Ruthless with Myself?

Of course, this is only the first challenge. Every step of the way the agent is going to be checking to be sure that you really are an investor and not a consumer. Why would the agent do this?

The reason is simple: the agent wants to make a sale and a good agent realizes that to do this, he or she must satisfy the buyer. Because the vast majority of people who buy homes to live in are consumers, the agent is going to be suspicious, wondering if you aren't really a consumer in disguise.

It's an important point for the agent. If he or she shows you a wonderful investment property and you say something such as, "I don't like the color of the living room" or "I don't think my TV will fit in the den," the agent has shown you the wrong kind of property and he or she won't get a sale. Thus the agent wants to know up front that when you see that really good investment property you'll instead say, "How much profit can I make when I resell?" The agent needs to be sure of your motives to get you what you really want.

You need to be sure of them, too. That's why you must be ruthless with yourself.

I can recall when my wife and I were looking at many investment properties. Very often when we would walk in she'd say something like, "Isn't that entranceway atrocious—I'd put in wallpaper instead of that horrible paint." I'd say, "Boy, would I like to have that garage with the extra room for the tool bench." We would tend to go through the house, alternatively condemning this or oohing and ahhing about that as we saw how the place would fit in with our own desires and needs.

But be assured, we are experienced buyers. After this little bit of self-indulgence, we would look at each other and one of us surely would say, "But we're not buying it for ourselves. We're buying it for investment." And then we'd go through a second time seeing it with totally different eyes. We're ruthless about our approach.

And so must you be. If you're fairly new to it, I suggest you keep off the consumer path entirely, lest you be tempted and begin backsliding. You want it for investment, strictly. There'll be plenty of time later on to consider whether or not you can stand to live in the place—you're not buying the instant you walk in. Better to insist on looking at it first as strictly an investment property. You'll keep from confusing your agent. And you'll keep your own mind straight.

How Can I Be Ruthless with the Seller?

Eventually, you'll find a good investment house, one that fits your budget, that has a financial back door out in case things go terribly wrong, and that offers a good chance of selling for a profit down the road. (We'll cover how to determine all of these in the next chapters.) So you make an offer and immediately you're into negotiating with the seller.

If it's a single-family house or condo or co-op, the seller is going to assume that you're buying it for pleasure—to live in yourself, to consume. This is going to color the seller's thinking significantly.

If the seller thinks the buyers are consumers, the seller is going to automatically assume that a significant portion of the offer is based not on cool-headed judgment but on emotion. The buyers must "like" something about the house. The buyers "desire" the property. The buyers "want" to move in and live there. In other words, the seller has some room to dicker with the price and terms. As a consumer, you might very well pay more (sometimes much more) than the house is worth considered strictly as an investment. Your offer, particularly if it's a lowball offer, might not be considered serious and the seller might counteroffer very high, which is definitely not to your advantage.

Therefore, it's important that if you don't directly submit your offer to the seller (something you may want to do), you have the agent convey the idea that the buyers are investors. They are looking at the house strictly from an investment perspective.

This usually causes sellers to sit back in their chairs and go "Oh." Now all of the arguments regarding how pretty the place is, how cozy, how comfortable, and so forth don't hold any water. It comes down to dollars and sense. The agent acting for you can point out comparables, appraisals, and market trends— whatever is useful to justify your price.

And the seller's only recourse is to say he or she will wait for a consumer type of buyer to come along, or acknowledge the reality of the situation and truly consider selling the place strictly for its investment value.

You want the seller to see you as a cold-hearted "ruthless" investor. You want the seller to believe that you don't care about that wonderful painted stone fireplace the seller labori- ously put in or the skylight that he overspent $5,000 on. You don't care anything about that. You're strictly a dollars-and- cents person. If the house is worth the money, you'll buy. If not, you'll look at three dozen other houses that will do just as well.

It's enough to make a seller sit up and consider. It may even be enough to convince him to accept a deal that he might not otherwise go for.

Of course, to pull this off, you must indeed be an investor, or at least your agent must be convinced you are. And for that to happen, for you to be convincing, you must believe it yourself.

Your agent, the seller, and you—all must believe you are a ruthless investor, *if* you're to buy right so you can sell high.

Will You Like What You Get?

But—and this is a serious question—what if you succeed? What if you find a good investment property and convince a seller to accept the right terms and price. And you buy it! Do you really want it?

Remember, this is still the place you're going to have to live in. This is still going to be your home. If it's the best investment in the world, you're not going to be happy with it if it just doesn't suit your needs and desires.

My suggestion is that you not worry too much about this problem.

We are all consummate consumers. We are born to it. No matter how much we try to act like investors, no matter how much we attempt to be ruthless, we're still going to be looking with our heart.

I can tell you right now that no matter how seriously you attempt to see a property from an investment perspective, just below the surface you're going to be judging it like a consumer. It's just as I noted earlier when my wife and I first see a house we want to purchase. We literally can't help ourselves. Automatically, we put ourselves in the property as if it were going to be our own home. And even though we force ourselves to see things as investors, just below the surface we are always considering, "Would our chest of drawers fit there?" Or "Will the children sleep together in one room or do we need an extra bedroom?"

I suspect the same may be true for you. As you force yourself to consider the property as an investment, a little voice is going to be constantly analyzing, asking whether or not this will really work out.

And just before you make the offer, you should stand back and listen carefully to that little voice. Before you write out a deposit check and sign a sales agreement, say to yourself, "Now, I've gotten to the point where I know that if the seller accepts, I've got a good deal. But do I really want it? Am I willing to live in this house for the time it's going to take to resell it?"

If the answer is "Yes," as it probably will be if your consumer radar is working at all, just go right ahead with the good deal you're working on. On the other hand, if the answer is "No," then don't go forward.

Remember, ultimately the two paths of the consumer and the investor must both arrive at the same goal: a home for you. You've got to live there. You've got to like it at least minimally. You've got to be happy with yourself.

If for whatever reason (the neighborhood, the layout, the size, the number of stories, the age, whatever) you just can't stand the property, don't buy it no matter how good an investment it may appear to be.

And don't be hard on yourself for pulling out, either. Remember, there are lots of fish in the sea. More than four million homes change hands in the United States each year. There's at least one (probably thousands) that will fit your bill exactly—both as an investment . . . and a great place to live.

---

*R*uthless Buyer Checklist

❑ Do you now ask agents to find you an "investment" ?

❑ Is your main concern for how much and how quickly you can resell?

❑ Do you explain you're going to reside there "temporarily"?

❑ Do you keep reminding yourself you're buying an investment?

❑ Have you stopped oohing and ahhing over the home's features?

❑ Do you let the sellers know that you're an investor?

❑ Do sellers know that you're ONLY interested in dollars?

❑ Do you let the seller know you're happy to look elsewhere?

❑ Will you be happy with the house if you get it?

If you didn't check many of the statements, you're a milque-toast. Go back out there and practice snarling in the mirror a few times. If you checked most, you're on the way, but be careful of backsliding. If you checked them all, let the seller beware—you're ruthless!

CHAPTER 4

Is There a Winning Location?

The first house I ever bought to live in with my family, I bought wrong. I made a mistake and paid for it dearly when it came time to resell. However, the lesson I learned kept me from making the same mistake ever again and by retelling this story, I hope it will help you from making a similar error.

I was recently married, had just landed a not-well-paying job, and had only a few bucks in the bank. But I was determined to purchase my own home and not rent (the typical American dream). Because I was so strapped for cash, I let price be my number-one priority. When I went looking, I informed agents that I wanted a house for no more than a certain amount and I named a very low figure. I also wanted an assumable loan (because I didn't have the income to qualify for a new loan) and a minimal down payment. Needless to say, that severely restricted the number of homes available to me.

An enterprising agent, however, eventually did find exactly what I was looking for, at least as I saw it. The sellers were willing to accept most of the down payment in the form of a second mortgage, the payments were low, and the price was reasonable.

When the agent first took my wife and I to see the house, we traveled a circuitous route and I remember asking why were going such a long way around. I was told that it was so that we could get a better picture of the neighborhood.

The neighborhood was modest, at best. Most houses were kept up, but a few lawns were let go and weeds could be seen popping up here and there. There was the occasional broken down car in a driveway. Looking at my wife, I realized she was a little taken aback by the area, but I felt quite good knowing that from a financial perspective, this would be a perfect house.

Indeed, the house itself was quite nice. The lot was well landscaped with a beautiful weeping willow tree in front. It had a nice backyard, the house was plenty big enough for us and it had a cute kitchen. We both loved it and happily talked about the purchase as we got back into the agent's car for the trip to his office, where we made the offer.

We offered lower than the seller was asking with more favorable terms to us and then left while the agent went off to try to secure the seller's signature. During the interim, we decided to drive past the house again. Only we couldn't find it. We spent nearly an hour twisting through different neighborhoods and streets, but we simply couldn't remember how to get there. I realized this was because of the strange route the agent had taken to show us the place and something gnawed at my mind . . . something just wasn't right, but I couldn't put my finger on it.

When we got back to the agent's office, we were astonished to hear that the seller had accepted our offer, exactly as we had made it, not one item changed. Again, this seemed strange, but I put it out of my mind. We had bought a house on our terms and I was delighted.

A month later we moved in. We now had a map and drove directly to our new home. We drove through dilapidated streets, broken-down homes with windows busted out, broken cars on almost every driveway, and refuse on the streets. My wife was actually afraid of the neighborhood. "Don't worry," I said, "This isn't where we live." We drove on, turned a corner, went down three houses and there was our new home, right on the edge of a terrible slum. The truth was, it was indeed where we lived.

I felt my face drop when I realized how close we were to a "bad" area. However, I perked up because I knew that we had paid a very low price, had gotten easy terms, and could well afford the payments.

We lived in that house for a little under a year. By itself, it was very nice. We had mostly nice neighbors. But, we did notice that the run-down area seemed to be creeping closer to us. Almost from the first week we were in the property, we realized we had made a mistake. Although we liked the house, we just didn't want to live where it was located.

Soon we put up the house for sale . . . and realized why the sellers who had sold it to us had taken our first offer. No one wanted to buy, because of the location. Many agents wouldn't even list our home!

However, I had at least been smart from a financial point of view. We had an assumable loan. By offering the house for nothing down, we eventually were able to find buyers (poor souls!) to take it off our hands. They simply took over the existing mortgage. We lost what down payment we had put into the property and we ended up paying off the second mortgage out of our own funds. But we were out!

I often reminisce about that home. It was definitely a mistake. But it also helped us to grow. That was more than 35 years and dozens of houses ago. We never ever made that mistake again. We have on many occasions bought houses that were, in reality, too expensive for us, or too big, or in need of too many repairs. But we have never ever bought a home that wasn't in a top neighborhood. And we have never had a problem reselling, quickly, and for good money.

How Do You Find a Good Neighborhood?

The moral of the story is obvious: get the right location and everything will take care of itself.

But what exactly does it mean to say the "right location"? Is it a neighborhood, a street, a school district, a shopping area—what makes for the right location?

Actually, seven factors should be carefully considered when we talk location:

1. Neighborhood

2. Growth

3. Schools

4. Crime

5. Access

6. Shopping

7. Competition

This may seem like a lot, but in reality it isn't. Several overlap. For example, while you're finding out about schools, you can also often check into crime statistics. Growth and competition from other areas go hand in hand as does access to transportation and shopping. However, we'll consider each of these separately.

What's a Good Neighborhood?

In Chapter 2 we talked about how an investor picks a neighborhood—by property value and potential appreciation. I suggest you do the same thing. Contact an agent who has access to a computerized listing system. Find out which neighborhoods in the area where you want to live consistently have higher sales levels and where prices have consistently gone up. (Often agents can tell you this information off the top of their head!) Then look *only* in these neighborhoods.

On the other hand, what if the search area is huge? I was recently asked by a young man who is just starting out how to limit his search. His problem was that because he worked out of his home, he could live within a fairly large geographical area. Because he was a resident of the Los Angeles area, he had several thousand square miles to choose from.

He had asked several agents which neighborhoods were best, but the trouble was, all the agents he talked with were "locals." They knew their own little area well enough, but knew little outside of it. In other words, he couldn't get a sense of where might be best to look—north, south, east, or west.

If this is your problem, you may want to consider taking more time and actually going to numerous different communities and speaking to agents in each of them. Be prepared for an agent in one area to slam or at least run down another area. The old truism that you tend to knock what you don't know applies here. But by roving around, you'll quickly get up to speed on a very big geographical area. Do it on weekends if possible over a couple of months. During the course of that time, you can easily come to learn a great deal about a half dozen or more different communities. And because you've been doing the traveling and the checking, you'll be developing a much better sense of which areas are doing better and which are worse.

In any event, follow the advice in Chapter 2. Locate the best areas in terms of price appreciation. Once you've done this, then check out each area.

You actually have two courses of action you need to take. First, you need to identify a suitable neighborhood. Second, you need to identify a good house within that neighborhood. Here's a quick checklist to help you get up to speed on finding a neighborhood and scouring it for the best house.

Does Growth Make a Difference?

There's the old story of John Jacob Astor who was America's first real estate tycoon back in the 1800s. His plan for success was simple. He lived in New York City. So he just went to the outskirts of the city in the direction it was growing and bought whatever he could, mostly farms and unwanted land. A few years later when developers came through, they bought from him, giving him a substantial profit. He kept doing this again and again, really a simple-minded approach, until he had acquired millions of dollars.

$\mathcal{Q}$uick Neighborhood and House Checklist

Yes **No**

☐ ☐ 1. Is there graffiti on walls?

Avoid neighborhoods with lots of graffiti. Regardless of what the price statistics show, chances are these are ready for a fall and they could take you with them.

☐ ☐ 2. Do the homes face busy streets?

In the more exclusive communities, the rear walls of the homes at the outside of the neighborhood face the busy street while all the fronts face inward toward quiet streets. This is much more desirable.

☐ ☐ 3. Is it a gated community?

Some builders' studies suggest that adding a gate to a neighborhood adds about 5 percent overall to values. Having a gate also adds a certain prestige to an area.

☐ ☐ 4. Is there heavy foliage?

People like neighborhoods that have tall trees and lots of shrubbery. They will pay more to live there and more quickly purchase such a property.

☐ ☐ 5. Is the house the smallest in the neighborhood?

Remember, you want to avoid the biggest house in the neighborhood. Chances are it is too big for most buyers and could be trouble reselling. Sometimes, however, a much smaller than average house can itself be a drawback. (It's probably too small for buyers who want the neighborhood.) Something a little smaller than average is ideal.

☐ ☐ 6. Are the surrounding houses in good condition?

Often people decide whether or not they'll buy a house not by the actual property itself but by its neighbors. Run-down houses suggest bad neighbors.

❏ ❏ 7. Is the house appropriate for the area?

Buyers with children like to see toys and bikes on a neighbor's front lawn. Retired people don't. Retirees like smaller homes, while families like bigger ones. A small house in an area with families is a hard sell as is a large home in a retirement area.

❏ ❏ 8. Is it a corner lot?

Corner lots only appear to give you more room. Usually, the extra space is in front in the form of lawns with less rear, private area. Corner lots cost more in maintenance and fewer people are interested in buying them.

❏ ❏ 9. Is it a "key" lot?

Key lots have the backs of two other lots adjoining them, instead of the back of just one other lot. They are usually next to a corner lot and are less desirable.

❏ ❏ 10. Is it a "view" lot?

A lot with a view is highly desirable and will always sell faster and for more money than a lot without a view. You may pay more going in, but you'll get more coming out.

❏ ❏ 11. Is it a "hole" lot?

A "hole" lot is one that has tall buildings or higher ground surrounding it. The house seems to be sunk into a hole. These are far less desirable and much harder to sell.

❏ ❏ 12. Is it a "low-maintenance" yard?

In suburban areas, built-in sprinklers, a drip system, small lawns, rock gardens, and so on are usually very desirable. The exception is a rural area where big yards with fruit trees may be desirable.

❏ ❏ 13. Does it have its own driveway?

Mutual or shared driveways are the kiss of death. Avoid them like the plague. You will always be fighting your neighbor over them and savvy buyers will refuse to consider the property when you want to resell.

❑   ❑   14. Does it have a circular driveway?

A circular driveway means that you drive in one entrance and out another. It is far more desirable than a straight driveway from which you have to back out.

❑   ❑   15. Is it a busy street?

Nobody likes a busy street. Buyers with children are particularly concerned about busy streets and may refuse to buy just for this reason.

❑   ❑   16. Is it fenced?

Some areas of the country don't have fences. But in those areas that do, a high-quality tall fence is desirable for privacy. In areas without fences, hedges and bushes often fulfill the same function.

❑   ❑   17. Does it have "curb appeal?"

"Curb appeal" refers to the first impression the home makes on a likely buyer. Some homes are set on a lot in such a way that they just look good when you first see them. Others look awkward, dull, homely, and so on. Remember, you can never remake a first impression. Homes with curb appeal sell faster and for more. (If you're not sure, have a friend drive by and give his or her opinion. You'll quickly find out.)

Can you do the same?

Today, it's not quite so simple. There are investors/speculators everywhere. Many know this tale well and spend a lot of time looking for undeveloped property in the direction of growth. Usually by the time you'll get to undeveloped land, it's all tied up. Besides, you're not interested in land, are you? Presumably, you want a house to live in.

Even with a single-family house (or a condo or co-op), however, growth—or the lack of it—remains a big factor.

Consider this true story. Sarah and Timothy each bought a home in the same year. Timothy bought in a well-developed tract in the center of a valley in which they both lived. The tract had been around for a good 20 years and the prices were well established. Sarah bought in a relatively new development at the outskirts of the valley in which they lived. There was little shopping or transportation out there. At the time, the prices they paid were within a few thousand dollars of each other.

However, growth was in Sarah's favor. An expressway was soon built through the area and shortly afterward, a new shopping center went up less than a mile away from her home. New schools and playgrounds likewise were built.

Five years after they both purchased, they both sold. Timothy received a small increase in value for his home. But Sarah's property had almost doubled in value.

Why the difference? The reason has to do with growth. Sarah's property was right in the path of growth and benefited from it. Timothy's property had been passed by. Growth boosted Sarah's profit.

Does the Desirability of a Location Change?

What's important here is to learn to begin thinking about the ownership of property not as a static thing, but as a progression over a period of time. What neighborhoods are today will very likely not be what they are tomorrow. Some get better, some get worse.

While it's hard to predict with any certainty what any given neighborhood will look like five or ten years down the road, buying in the direction of growth helps enormously. If a community is growing, it's safe to say that property in the direction of growth will appreciate the fastest. Just as in the case of Astor, simply buying a home in the right location (the direction of growth) and waiting may be all that it takes to make your fortune in real estate!

How Do You Know in Which Direction a Community May Be Growing?

You can ask real estate agents. Most know exactly and can quickly tell you. You can check with lenders. Although they are not supposed to treat one neighborhood differently from another, most know exactly which direction growth is going. You can call your local newspaper and ask to speak to someone who writes for the real estate section. Strike up a conversation, explain why you're interested, and chances are you'll get a highly researched answer in a few minutes. If you really can't find out, check at the business department of any local college or university. You're likely to find at least one professor who specializes in real estate and can give you a very erudite explanation of which way the community is growing.

What About "No Growth"?

Be aware, however, that not all communities grow! Many are stagnant with little to no growth over a period of years and even decades. Typically, these are rural areas where there are no large industries spurring growth or they are older urban areas where industries have packed up and left and there is actually negative growth.

Also be aware that sometimes the direction of growth changes. This generally happens as old industries leave and new ones come in, in other locations.

Finding out the direction of growth may take a bit of effort. Generally, only investors take the time and energy. But if you do, and then buy in the right direction, you'll find that you've maximized your chances of owning a property that appreciates rapidly and sells readily.

How Much Do Schools Count?

By some estimates, the single biggest factor in determining the appreciation of homes within an area is the quality of its schools. Homes that feed into high-quality schools appreciate in value. Those with poor schools don't.

Can it be just that simple?

Of course, there are other factors. But only a fool would overlook the influence that schools have. (Certainly, no investor would overlook it!) The majority of home buyers have children and they are looking to get their children into the best schools possible. This is especially true with the way in which schools in most areas of the country have declined in quality and safety.

Today, good schools are the exception more than the rule and as a result, a home in an area with a high-quality school program is likely to command more money and be resold quicker.

How do you find out whether or not schools in an area are good or not so good? Again, first ask your agent. This is such an important issue that most agents keep up-to-date information on it.

However, sometimes agents don't know or are behind the times in their assessment. Therefore, after you've picked a neighborhood, take a few minutes to call the local school district and ask about national and state scholastic test scores. These are almost always available. Check them out. Schools at the 80th percentile and higher are generally quite good. Watch out for schools that are below the 50th-percentile rank.

Also be aware that sometimes schools excel in one grade level and fall down in another. Scores may be high in elementary school but way off in middle and high school. Or it may be the other way around. Ask to see *all* the scores, not just the ones for the grade levels in which your children will attend the next year. (Remember, while you may be interested only in elementary school today, eventually your child will be going to high school.)

Finally, be aware that school districts also change over time. Some grow better, others become less effective. However, a good indication of how well any school district will fare in the future is funding. Is the community willing to pass tax-revenue bond issues for schools? Check county records and, once again, ask your agent. Bond issues mean higher property taxes, which is a drawback in an age of downsizing. However, any high taxes you pay will be more than offset in property appreciation because of good schools. If the community has consistently passed school revenue bonds, it's an excellent portent for the future. If these bonds have regularly been turned down, watch out for the area. It could be headed downhill in the future.

How Big an Issue Is Crime?

That depends on how bad the crime is.

Today, many people consider crime the number-one problem in the country. They worry about it. And when they purchase a home, they act on their worries.

That's the reason that gated communities have sprung up everywhere, and are in such high demand. As noted previously, the general rule is that a home in a gated community will sell faster and for more, just because it's gated.

Be aware, however, that in many cases the "gate" is nothing more than a cosmetic device designed to attract homebuyers. Often anyone can get around these gates (particularly if no guards are posted). Check out the device to be sure it works well and that it does the job it was intended to do.

Also, whether or not you are considering a gated community, check out the crime statistics for the area. The local police department will have statistics on the incidence of murder, rape, arson, burglary, and so on. See how the statistics for the area you are considering compare with other areas.

While being located in the safest area in the state may not necessarily add much to the value of property, being situated in one of the worst areas will definitely detract from it. In other words, you want a relatively crime-free area to maintain property values, not necessarily to increase them. You want to avoid high-crime areas because this one factor can cause values to drop.

Should I Watch Out for Access?

A few years ago I lived in quite a nice area of Los Angeles called Palos Verdes. It's a kind of a huge rock jutting out into the Pacific Ocean and forming a shallow peninsula. It's tall, almost 1,500 feet, and it has a very large shoreline with thousands of homes with excellent views. Away from the shoreline are huge lots, big enough to raise horses. Needless to say, this is the type of community where you'd expect prices to be high and appreciation strong. And they are.

Except for one factor that both limits and defines the area—access. There are no freeways near Palos Verdes, even today. And in a part of the country where freeway access is the lifeblood of the community, this is definitely a drawback.

From the oceanside of "PV," it takes a good half hour to reach a major freeway. Then it takes however long on the freeway (often highly congested) to get to where you're going.

The result is that those who must commute to work for a living find it very difficult to reside in this community. There are, of course, a few industries nearby, but these do not provide nearly as many jobs as there are homes.

As a result, one would expect that prices and appreciation would be held down "on the rock." And to some extent they are.

However, many of the homeowners bought years ago and are retired. They enjoy the privacy that lack of freeways brings as well as the seaside atmosphere. As a result, they do not move often and fewer properties are offered for sale than might otherwise be expected from such a large area. And as a result, the problem of lack of access tends to be overcome by scarcity and prices stay high and do appreciate.

I've chosen the peninsula as an example because it illustrates several aspects of how access to a neighborhood influences value. Taken by itself, lack of access is a definite negative. However, if the community has some type of anchor to make it attractive—in this case proximity to the ocean—the negative can actually become a positive.

Therefore, when you're considering a purchase, look closely at access. Simple lack of it isn't enough to make the case that the community should be discarded from your search. Maybe lack of access has become a plus. On the other hand, having very easy access may only mean that most people who live there work far away, creating a bedroom community that may be too dependent on distant industries.

When gauging access, the things to look for in terms of proximity are:

- Freeways (expressways, thruways, whatever they're called in your area)

- Public transportation (buses, subways, trains, and so on)

- Distance to a major airport (lots of people commute by plane or take frequent business flights)

- Wide, easily traveled (not congested) streets within the community leading to uncongested freeways, public transportation, and so on

- Speed limits on streets (It doesn't help to have a wide street if you must travel 10 miles on it and the speed limit is only 25 miles per hour.)

Sometimes you can be fooled by access. For example, there may be a major station for a subway or train line within a few miles of the neighborhood. You may think that this means that anyone living here can easily take a car to the station, park it, and then ride the subway or train to work.

However, it may turn out that the station is inadequate to handle all the commuters who want to use it. Its parking lot may fill up with cars by five in the morning and after that, there's no place to park. Surrounding neighborhoods, affected by parking on the streets, may have enacted ordinances to prevent commuters from leaving their cars in the neighborhood during the day.

This type of congestion is common in many areas and may be enough to steer potential buyers away from the area. Lack of access to public transportation can be a limiting factor on the growth of a community and on appreciation of home prices.

Or there may be a freeway on-ramp only a few blocks from the neighborhood. That looks good. But in the mornings it may be so crowded and the freeway so stacked up, that many would-be commuters are discouraged from using it. Once again, lack of access caused by congestion may limit values in the community.

My suggestion is that when you are considering access, you take the time to determine how viable it is. Go there one morning and try to park in the train station. Or attempt to get on the freeway from the local on-ramp. See how tight things really are. And let your observation help determine your purchase.

(Keep in mind that if you buy in a growth area, as noted previously, today's easy access might turn out to be tomorrow's congestion. Growth communities do just what they say—grow. And more people mean more demand for access.)

Is Nearby Shopping a Necessity?

In an age of automobiles, nearby shopping is no longer a necessity. The days when the homemaker walked to the store every day for fresh food are mostly gone.

However, some nearby shopping is very nice. A grocery store, drug store, hardware store, and restaurant that can be reached by walking, or least by a short five-minute car ride, enhance a neighborhood. If they are absent, when it comes time to resell, any potential buyer has to feel negative about the lack of shopping. And too many negatives mean it's a hard resell. What you usually want is a small shopping center with these stores and a couple of good restaurants nearby.

On the other hand, too much shopping can detract from a property's value. I can recall looking at homes in one neighborhood over a period of nearly ten years. The area backed up to a major mall. Those houses who had yards right up against the mall actually went down in value. The entire neighborhood, however, was affected and showed slow growth, this at a time when other most distant neighborhoods were shooting up in value.

Avoid property right next to huge shopping areas. The noise, the light, and the congestion are considered quite unappealing to many buyers.

What about Competition from Other Homes?

This is an issue too often overlooked by homebuyers. Again, it's a factor of time. What you see today will not last forever. And tomorrow's reality may cause neighborhood values to decline.

Consider the case of a home that a friend owned in Northern California. This house was located in a pleasant valley, close (but not too close) to shopping, with good schools, and good freeway access. Price appreciation had been steady and strong for at least the previous ten years. In fact, it had everything going for it. So my friend bought.

Within a year, however, developers began work on housing in the next valley over. They began building an amazing 7,000 new homes. The newer properties were competitively priced, but they had better financing. And their neighborhoods had wider streets, community recreation and parks, green belts and hiking trails. In short, the newer community was in many ways far superior to the older one. Furthermore, because of the homes' impact on the freeways, the access from my friend's neighborhood became congested.

As soon as the new homes went up for sale, agents began reporting that buyers couldn't be found for homes in my friend's older community. Nobody wanted to buy there. Everyone seemed to want to buy in the new community. (We'll have more to say about buying older homes versus newer ones in a later chapter.)

Two years after moving in, my friend had to sell because of a job change. To her chagrin she discovered that prices in her neighborhood had not gone up. Indeed, they had actually drifted lower. By the time she paid commission and closing costs, she would lose money!

What caused the problem? Competition. The new homes in the next valley over stole the buyers that would otherwise have purchased my friend's house. She had trouble selling—it took a long time and she lost money—because she hadn't bothered to consider competing homes.

The moral here is that when you buy, you should also check to see whether there are going to be competing houses built nearby. If there are, perhaps you would be better off waiting and then buying one of those!

The same holds true for condominiums (including town-houses) and stock co-operatives. Is there competition on the horizon? If so, then perhaps you might want to wait for it.

How Do You Determine If There's Going to Be Competition?

It can be difficult. What we're talking about is not necessarily something you can drive by and see. If today you drive by where competition will be tomorrow, you may only see cows grazing on open land as they have for decades. It doesn't suggest much of a threat.

However, land can be cleared and a large development can be built within months. Where cows grazed yesterday, tomor-row families can be living in split-level homes and children can be playing and going to school.

To find out, you have to check with the local planning commission (department or whatever the office is called in your area). Usually it only takes a trip to the service counter and a few words with one of the staff. While it takes only months to build new homes, it usually takes years to get approval. Just say you're thinking of buying in the area and want to know what new housing developments are seeking approval.

If there are any, you should be quickly told.

Next, ask how long it usually takes to get approval and how long these developments have been seeking it. You might also ask if the developers have run into any special problems that are delaying (or possibly derailing) the developments.

Within a few minutes you should have all the details on developments as much as five years in the future.

Note

This is one area where I wouldn't necessarily rely on an agent. Many agents simply won't know. Others may pooh-pooh any concerns, saying something such as, "I've been here for 20 years and we haven't seen any new developments."

Maybe, but that doesn't mean that next year one won't come along. Take the time to check it out with the planning department. (If you don't want to go to the department, at least make a call. It won't take more than 15 minutes and could make a huge difference when it comes time to resell.)

These, then, are the seven factors to consider when looking for a winning location. To repeat, they are:

1. Neighborhood—check area and location of house

2. Growth—be in the right direction

3. Schools—get high quality, worth the extra money

4. Crime—go for gated communities and low graffiti

5. Access—seek easy on/off freeways, train stations

6. Shopping—you want a little, too much is bad

7. Competition—watch out for the future

---

*C*hecklist for Location

❏ Have you asked more than one agent about areas?

❏ Are you buying in the direction of growth?

❏ Have you checked out the local schools?

❏ Have you asked neighbors about the schools and crime?

❏ Have you asked the police about crime statistics?

❏ Did the location pass the "graffiti" test?

❏ Can you easily get to a freeway or train station?

❏ Can you easily get to nearby shopping?

❏ Are they building competitive new homes nearby?

Check only a few and chances are you're going to lose money when you resell. Check most and you should at least break even. Check them all and you should be very happy with your profits.

Now that we've checked out the neighborhood, let's consider what to look for in the home itself.

CHAPTER 5

Is There a Better House Design?

A few years ago I was looking for a home and came across one that was unique—it was round!

I don't know about you, but I hadn't seen too many round houses before. I made a point of visiting it, just to satisfy my curiosity.

The selling agent just nodded as I went through, part of a steady stream of agents and buyers who were looking at the home. Apparently, we were *all* nothing more than curious!

The problem with a round design became immediately apparent. The property didn't have any square rooms. Either the rooms were pie shaped, or they had many unusual angles. As a result, the living centers tended to be large and awkward and the bedrooms small and cramped. Needless to say, this wasn't the type of house I'd like to live in. Apparently, most people agreed. The owner, who had built it, had to keep reducing the price until someone finally bought it to use as a rental. And as I heard, even that investor had trouble finding tenants!

The point is that the design itself can either enhance a property's chances of resale or detract from them. A wise buyer, trying to look at property through the eyes of an investor (even though intending to live there) is far better off getting a "popular" design than one that is unique, unusual, and, as a result, less desirable.

Do the Numbers Work?

Think of it in terms of numbers. For every buyer of a round home, there are probably a hundred buyers for more conventional homes. This means that the seller of the round home has to get 100 times more buyers, on average, to look at the property to get one to make an offer. Would you rather be selling a round home or a square one? (In a very real sense, reselling is just a matter of getting enough buyers to walk through the property. The more potential buyers who see the home and the more appealing it is, the quicker you're going to get a successful sale.)

You can even plot the appeal of a home on a graph. In the following chart, the top and bottom represent unique properties, usually those that some individual designed and built to suit personal tastes or needs. The center represents the more common properties, typically those designed and built by leading developers.

For this graphic presentation, "1" represents the least desirable home, "9" the most desirable. The higher the number, the more potential buyers are available.

You want the property *you* buy to be a "9." You don't want it to be a "1."

What Is a "Popular Design"?

Having established that the more popular a home's design, the easier it will be to find buyers, the next question becomes: what makes for a popular design? While round may be out, what about square versus rectangle or two stories versus one?

Over the years, a number of builders have attempted to conduct informal surveys to determine what features are important to buyers and what are negatives. In looking over these

---

*P*roperty Appeal

1
22
55555
88888888
99999999999999999999
88888888
55555
22
1

---

surveys, I find that they are based mostly on just common sense. Buyers like big rooms. They want convenient kitchens. Bathrooms should be modern and so on.

To help you determine what to look for that will be popular in a home design, I've come up with my own list, compiled after examining many other lists and talking with hundreds of buyers and agents. No, it's not scientific, but I think it's very close to what people are thinking of today.

In addition to the suggestions from the checklist, a house that you're considering should have other features as well that will make it easier to resell. In a later chapter, for example, we'll consider the size of the home. For now, however, here are other areas to watch for.

Note

Whims and desires change over time. Back in the 1950s, hardwood floors were a big issue. Today, hardly anyone cares. (Hardwood has become so expensive that it is prohibitive as flooring material in all but the most expensive properties.) Use the following checklist with a grain of salt and remember that you will want to resell sometime in the future—not today. Thus, a large of part of your selection will be guesswork about what future buyers will like.

$\mathcal{H}$ome Design Checklist

Yes No

❏   ❏   1. Is the master bedroom in front?

It's a matter of noise. Houses with front master bedrooms tend to be less desirable because of street noise. Rear bedrooms tend to be quieter. Of course, this generality may not always be true. If the back of the house faces a rec center, the opposite may be the case.

❏   ❏   2. Is the master bedroom isolated from the entertainment areas?

Again, it's a matter of noise. An isolated master bedroom is more preferable. A master bedroom off a kitchen is the least desirable. Master bedrooms off living rooms and family rooms are also less desirable because of their awkward access.

❏   ❏   3. Is it one story?

The elderly and families with small children often prefer single-story homes because of the difficulty in climbing stairs. Young adult couples often prefer two stories because of the isolation of upstairs bedrooms from entertainment centers downstairs. The rule here is to take a look at the neighborhood and make sure the number of stories matches the likely composition. Don't get a two-story home in a retirement community, for example.

❏   ❏   4. Does it have long, dark hallways?

Long, dark hallways are the sign of poorly designed houses. They are universally disliked. Some hallway area may be unavoidable, but it should be short and well lit.

❏   ❏   5. Is the kitchen large and airy?

Kitchens often sell (and resell) the house. Larger kitchens are in vogue these days. Kitchens with "island" counter space are particularly desirable. The kitchen should have lots of window area as well as good lighting.

❏   ❏   6. Are the appliances new and of good quality?

Kitchen appliances are scrutinized by buyers. Their quality often suggests the overall quality of the home. Replacing old, worn-out appliances with new high-quality ones can be very expensive.

❏   ❏   7. Does it have at least two bathrooms?

Houses with one bathroom are no longer acceptable. Three bathrooms are preferable, but two are an absolute minimum. Each must have a sink, toilet, and either a shower or a tub.

❏   ❏   8. Does it have at least three bedrooms?

Three bedrooms seems to be the absolute minimum. Even for just a couple, three seems the magic number—a master bedroom (with a bath off of it), a study/office/workroom, and a guest bedroom. A home with less than three bedrooms is often considered deficient.

❏   ❏   9. Does it have more than four bedrooms?

On the other hand, too many bedrooms are often considered wasted and unusable space. No one wants to pay for something they aren't going to use and homes with too many bedrooms often fill that bill. A fourth bedroom (the extra often converts to a den) is usually considered a nice feature. Five or more bedrooms is considered limiting the house to be resalable only to a large family.

❏   ❏   10. Does it have at least a two-car garage?

One-car garages are no longer acceptable. More desirable is extra room in the garage for a workbench or a three-car garage.

❏   ❏   11. Does it have a swimming pool?

If it does, avoid it. A home with a pool in excellent condition is, indeed, easier to resell. But pool maintenance is very high. And sometimes pools will crack or develop problems that are incredibly expensive to fix. Attempting to sell a home with a problem pool is very, very difficult. Better not to have a pool at all, than to take a chance on a pool developing a problem over your tenure of ownership.

❏   ❏   12. Does it have a spa?

In many parts of the country, home spas are considered almost a necessity. A spa definitely will help sell the house, and maintenance, if continued on a regular basis, can be minimum. Also, spa problems are far fewer than pool problems.

❏   ❏   13. Does it have air-conditioning?

In the warmer and muggier areas of the country, air-conditioning is a necessity, not an option. Homes without air-conditioning will sell for less and take longer to sell.

❏   ❏   14. Does it have an entryway?

Homes with entries or front porches are more desirable than those where the front door opens right onto the front yard. The reasons include extra privacy and more luxurious appearance.

❏ ❏ 15. Does it have an expensive-looking front door?

The quality of the front door (and door handle/lock) set the tone for the rest of the house. A high-quality door bespeaks a high-quality home. Replacing front doors can be expensive.

❏ ❏ 16. Is the heating system economical?

No one wants to spend a lot of money heating a house. In fact, many buyers will refuse to make offers on homes that have expensive heating systems. Electrical is the most expensive. Gas- or oil-fired circulating heaters, high-tech furnaces, and wood-burning stoves are the least expensive.

❏ ❏ 17. Is the house well insulated?

In both hot and cold climates, insulation is a necessity, not an option. The quality of insulation goes along with the heating system in determining heating/cooling costs. Look for high "R" ratings for insulation in ceilings (above R30 is good), in walls, and under floors (above R19 is good). Also, look for double-pane windows and insulation around the doors.

❏ ❏ 18. Does it have upgrades?

Unless the home was custom built, the builder/developer generally followed a "standard" plan. Usually, these standard plans offer the minimum with regard to features such as sinks, toilets, showers, countertops, flooring, and so forth. However, first owners will sometimes upgrade. They'll install tile instead of formica, more expensive bathroom fixtures, fancier lights, etc. While it's difficult to assess the actual increase in value these features add to a property, all together they work to make the home far more desirable.

Is the Roof in Good Shape?

All roofs wear out, some sooner, some later. Here's a list of the approximate lifetimes of different types of roofs.

Wood shingle	15 to 20 years
Heavy shake shingle	25 to 35 years
Asphalt/fiberglass	10 to 35 years (depending on quality and weather conditions)
Aluminum	50 years (depending on maintenance)
Cement/plastic	35 to 50 years
Tile	50 to 80 years (depending on maintenance)

If you buy a brand-new home, chances are you'll never have to worry about the roof. (Unless the builder did a bad job and it leaks!) The roof should last more than long enough for you to resell the property.

If you buy a resale, however, particularly one that's more than 15 years old, this presents another situation. The roof you're getting may be pretty worn out, and to resell, you may need to replace it. Roof replacements can be expensive, often costing $10,000 or more depending on the roofing material used.

Be sure to have a roof inspection so you'll know the roof's condition. If the roof needs to be replaced, negotiate to have the seller pay at least part of the replacement cost. Otherwise, when you go to resell, you'll have to pay the entire cost.

Is the Carpeting in Good Shape?

People tend to look down more than up. Thus, often the first thing a buyer sees when entering a home is the flooring. (If you doubt this, check it out in the next home you inspect.)

The better the flooring, the richer, more luxurious, and more desirable the home. So, when it comes time to resell, you want to be sure the flooring will look good.

Today, while hardwood and tile floors are still available in many houses, wall-to-wall carpeting is the rule. (If you buy a house with tile, be sure the tiles aren't cracked or if they are, you are able to buy replacements, which is not always easy. With hardwood floors, be sure that they are thick enough to take another sanding and finishing.) What you need to be concerned about is not so much what the carpeting looks like today, but what it will look like when you resell.

Brand-new, good-quality carpeting looks good for about five years, not usually any longer. This is not to say the carpeting isn't still usable, just that after about five years almost any carpeting begins to look rather bedraggled.

Therefore, if you're buying today and you get brand new carpeting, figure that you'll be able to resell with that flooring for about five years. After that, you'll have to bear the cost of replacing it (usually quite expensive.)

If you buy a place with older carpeting that is just getting by, figure that no matter when you sell, to get top dollars and a quick sale, you'll need to replace the flooring.

Don't underestimate the value good flooring adds to a property. As noted previously, buyers look down first. And often they continue to look there. Good flooring may cost thousands of dollars, but it can adds tens of thousands of dollars (plus a quicker sale) when you need to resell.

Are the Ceilings in Good Shape?

No, the ceilings are not so important as the carpets and you can get away with a lot more. But the ceilings do matter. Ceilings that have not been painted or redone in a long while tend to look brown or gray and make the home itself look drab. On the other hand, a fresh coat of paint or a freshly blown acoustical ceiling can pep up the appearance of a home. This is particularly the case in rooms that are not well lit.

Painting a ceiling (that has a flat surface) is just a matter of a bit of paint and little elbow grease. When you buy a home with this kind of a ceiling, don't worry too much about paint. When you go to resell, you can undoubtedly handle it yourself.

On the other hand, blown-in ceilings require professional work. You need an expert to either repaint or reblow them. If the ceiling is in mediocre shape when you buy the property, figure that five or so years down the road, it will be in unacceptable shape. Then you'll have to pop for the big bucks to have it redone so you can resell. Better to have this done by the person who sells it to you!

Are the Window Coverings in Good Shape?

Drapes and shades tend to wear out, get stained, get bleached by the sun, or otherwise need replacing. Even if they look good when you buy, they are something you probably will have to redo to resell down the road.

The above holds true unless you have shutters. Good wooden, metal, or plastic shutters last almost indefinitely. Yes, it's a minor point. (You can shutter the interior of a house for a few thousand dollars or less.) But as long as you're buying, why not find a home with good window coverings to begin with?

*C*hecklist for Design

❑ Will you give up your wants to get a popular design?

❑ Do you avoid long and dark hallways?

❑ Is the kitchen large and airy?

❑ Is the roof in good repair?

❑ Will the carpeting still look good by the time you resell?

❑ If there are floor tiles, are they cracked?

❑ If cracked, can you find replacements to match?

❑ Do the ceilings need to be repainted or resprayed?

❑ Will the window coverings last through a future resale?

Again, few checks and you're thinking too narrowly. Many checks and you'll probably end up with a resalable house. Check them all and you may actually be too intent on getting an investment—back off! You also need to be able to live in the place.

CHAPTER 6

Watch Out for Toxic Homes

This is a rather new issue these days and one that can be immensely important to you as a buyer. The reason is that today we're in a transition period between not caring if a home is environmentally safe and caring to the point of requiring a home to be nontoxic. Thus, you may buy today without really considering a home's toxicity only to find, several years down the road, that the next batch of buyers won't consider your home unless you spend upward of tens of thousands of dollars to detoxify it! So today's wise buyer, with an eye toward resale, is going to be very concerned about the environmental safety of any home purchase.

What Is a Toxic Home?

How, you may reasonably ask, can a home be toxic?

The answer is that any home that threatens its occupants is considered toxic. Here are some ways that a home may be toxic:

- Contains radon gas
- Has lead paint

- Has asbestos ceilings (or exposed asbestos elsewhere)

- Is not earthquake (hurricane) secured (or retrofitted)

- Has some other toxic element inside

Let's consider each of these potentially toxic features separately.

What's the Danger from Radon Gas?

Radon is essentially an odorless, colorless gas that in sufficient quantities is toxic to humans. It occurs naturally in certain ground formations and can rise up from the ground and accumulate typically in basements or lower floors of homes.

In certain areas of the country where radon is a problem, purchasers often require radon inspections of homes to check for accumulations of the gas. Typically, a home that has high radon levels will simply become unsalable, until the property is detoxified.

Checking for radon gas usually involves having a sensor device placed in a home for a period of time. A homeowner (or buyer) can do this and then have the sensor sent off to a lab for analysis. Generally, this process takes a month or so and costs around $50. Or a professional inspection can be made for more money and less time.

Correcting for radon can be difficult or easy, depending on the concentration and the speed at which it accumulates. Sometimes simply providing more air vents to a basement will be enough. Other times, it may be necessary to install an expensive blower system. It is possible that radon could be occurring so quickly and in such high levels that almost nothing will work.

Even if I weren't personally concerned about radon gas, I would attempt to determine if it were a problem in the area in which I was buying. (Most agents could tell you immediately if radon is a concern in the area.) If it was, I would insist on a radon inspection and a radon-free house, making the seller pick up the costs. The reason is that the next buyer, a few years down the road, will undoubtedly be just as concerned and make such a demand on me. And I don't want to have any problems or extra expenses when I resell.

Does the House Have Lead Paint?

Although roughly three-quarters of all homes built prior to 1978 contained lead paint (it was banned nationally in that year), lead paint in homes was not a big issue for most buyers and sellers until 1996. Then the federal government issued new disclosure requirements that suddenly thrust lead paint into the forefront of home sales. As time goes on, because of the current disclosure laws (and possibly tighter regulations in the future), it will become an increasingly larger issue.

Prior to 1978, lead was commonly added to most paints. It made painting easier and hid (concealed the undercovering) better. However, lead is one of the more toxic substances known to man. Thus, having lead in paint is considered a hazard.

Why Is Lead in Homes Toxic?

It has only been in the modern age that the toxicity of lead has been known. The more prosperous ancient Romans, for example, used lead pipes to bring water into their homes. As a result of drinking water tainted with lead, the well-heeled Romans were often more ill than their less well-off brethren. Indeed, a common drink enjoyed by the aristocracy was wine laced with lead. (The wine was allowed to steep in a lead goblet until it produced a particular taste that the Romans enjoyed.) This may have led to the mental illness that afflicted families of the Roman elite.

Today, lead paint in homes can produce lead poisoning when it is either ingested or inhaled. Small children sometimes chew on windowsills or door moldings. They can become ill if the paint on those areas contains lead.

Similarly, lead paint can chip off the outside of homes and impregnate the soil near the perimeter of a home. If this soil is ingested by small children, it can also lead to lead poisoning. And older paint will sometimes oxidize and turn to dust that can be scraped off (or in extreme cases blown off). This dust may contain particles of lead that when inhaled or ingested can be toxic.

There are many symptoms of lead poisoning, possibly the most well known being an apparent reduction in mental capacity. The symptoms mimic other diseases and usually a blood test is required to determine if a child or adult has toxic levels of lead in his or her bloodstream.

Because the vast majority of homes in the United States were built prior to 1978 and because most of us grew up in homes of that period, and because most of us don't have lead poisoning, the entire issue was considered moot by most of us. According to government statistics, however, as many as 1 in 11 children (almost 1.7 million) do have some level of lead poisoning. Removing lead from the home environment, therefore, has become a number-one priority for the Environmental Protection Agency (EPA).

As an aside, a secondary lead hazard in homes comes from the lead solder used to solder copper pipes together. Prior to about ten years ago, lead solder was commonly used. More recently, it has been banned for any potable water source. It has been known to leach out of soldered fittings and enter the water supply of homes.

This, however, is not quite so terrible as it first sounds. Lead leaching into water pipes usually is only in minimal amounts and then mostly when the water stands in the pipes for some time. This typically occurs only during the first five years of use. By then, most of the lead solder that comes in contact with water (actually a minute amount) has leached its lead out and very little remains.

If you're concerned, I've seen recommendations that you run the tap water for at least 30 seconds before filling your glass to take a drink. This allows the standing water in the pipes to clear out. (Older homes typically contain galvanized steel pipes and, therefore, do not have this particular problem.)

What Are the Current Disclosure Requirements?

When you go to buy a home that was built prior to 1978, the seller, today, must provide you with a federal disclosure statement telling you whether there are any known lead paints in the house. (Some states have their own disclosure statements.) You then have ten days to reconsider your purchase.

The current disclosure rules do not require that the seller have a professional inspection conducted to determine whether or not there is lead in the home (something that usually costs between $250 and $500). However, as a buyer you can order, and pay for, such an inspection yourself.

Furthermore, the current laws do not require the seller to remove lead paint if it is discovered. The seller only has to disclose it to you, the buyer. You then have the option of proceeding with the purchase as is, insisting on the seller removing the lead, paying for its removal yourself, or not buying the property.

Today, most people really aren't that concerned about the lead paint in a home. After all, as previously noted, most of us grew up with lead paint all around us and did not have a problem with it. By more carefully watching our children to see they don't chew on the house, we tend to feel fairly safe with it around. (Many people paint over old paint that has oxidized and is beginning to dust off to stabilize it; however, the EPA does not recommend encapsulation of lead paint as a solution.)

What Are the Likely Future Problems of Lead Paint?

Even with current disclosures, when we buy today we are not likely to be too concerned about lead paint. When we go to resell a few years down the road, however, we may wish we had paid more attention.

As time passes, more and more buyers will have grown up living in homes built after 1978. They will have grown up in an essentially lead-free environment and will be more concerned than most of us are about living in a home with lead paint. Increasingly, they will want to have the lead paint removed.

In addition, we should regard today's government disclosure requirements not as the final word on the subject but rather as only a first step. The EPA considers lead to be one of the top environmental hazards in the country. It is probably safe to say that a few years down the road the EPA may revise its disclosure requirements to make a professional inspection for lead paint mandatory. Eventually, the government could require all sellers to remove lead paint from a home before completing a sale! (This strict a measure is probably years down the road, if ever.)

Thus, if you're looking at a house today with an investor's eyes (considering resale), you would be well advised to consider the lead problem. While it may not affect your purchase, it could have severe financial repercussions later when you go to resell.

How Much Does It Cost to Remove Lead Paint?

The problem with lead paint removal is that the EPA does not recommend that the average homeowner do the work. The concern is that in the process of removal, more lead can be released as dust into the air. (For example, an ordinary vacuum cleaner will suck up lead dust, but the particles are so small that they may pass through the paper liner in the vacuum cleaner bag and be reintroduced into the air.)

Therefore, professionals are usually required to remove lead paint. And that spells money. Depending on how extensive the lead-paint use is, the cost can be anywhere from a few hundred dollars (for removing some old molding painted with lead paint) to removing all the paint inside and outside of the house at a price often exceeding ten thousand dollars!

Can You Have the Seller Pay for the Cost of Lead-Paint Inspection and Removal?

Probably not at the present time. Most sellers will pooh-pooh the whole idea and when they learn of the costs will prefer to refuse your offer and instead accept an offer from another buyer who doesn't make such demands.

However, as time goes by and lead paint in the home becomes an increasingly larger issue, more and more buyers will insist on its removal and eventually sellers will be forced to pay for at least a portion of the cleanup, just to be able to sell the property.

It strikes me that if you're a wise buyer today, at the least you will insist on an inspection to determine just how much lead paint there is in the property and thus determine what your potential liability could be. And once the inspection is made, the seller will have to reveal to all future buyers that the house does, indeed, contain lead paint. At this point you might be able to negotiate with the seller to pay at least a large portion of the removal costs.

Furthermore, if it turns out that there's lots of lead paint (particularly the case with much older homes), you may want to pass on the purchase or at least have the seller reduce the price somewhat to compensate for your likely future costs in having it removed.

In any event, simply ignoring the issue will not make it go away. As a buyer purchasing with investor's eyes, you will want to treat lead paint in the home quite seriously.

What about Asbestos Ceilings?

Many older homes also may have an asbestos problem. This can be in the form of insulation used years ago around heating pipes. This is often found in ductwork hidden in walls or located in basements. As long as no one is where the problem is, it's probably not a big concern.

Of more concern is likely to be textured (sometimes called "acoustical") ceilings blown into homes. Decades ago, the material used for these ceilings typically contained some asbestos.

The problem is that the ceiling can release small amounts of asbestos containing dust that can drift down and then be inhaled. However, most of the ceilings stabilize after a few years and unless they are disturbed, they release relatively small amounts of dust, if any at all. If you are concerned, tests can be performed on the air in a home having such ceilings to see if it contains asbestos, although these tests tend to be fairly expensive.

As with lead, removal usually requires professionals and is quite expensive. (Typically, the ceilings are wet down, thus removing the dust hazard, and then scraped.) Many times homeowners will have the ceilings resprayed (modern textured ceiling spray does not use asbestos) or repainted, thus encapsulating the old asbestos texture. This may not be an approved method.

Currently, there are no similar federal disclosure laws regarding asbestos in the home, although several states are looking into them. As with lead, it is something that a wise buyer considering future resale will want to check into very carefully.

What about Earthquake/Hurricane Securing or Retrofitting?

Many existing homes are simply not built to withstand the pressures the elements in their area may throw at them. For example, some homes in San Francisco and other parts of

California are simply built on mudsills. These are redwood planks laid on the ground that serve as a foundation.

Because some of these houses have lasted 80 years or more, we can't say that this is bad construction. However, we are talking about earthquake country and experience has shown that a sizable shaker can shift these homes off their foundation and cause them to tumble down.

Similarly, older homes in other areas of the country, notably where there are hurricanes, twisters, and other severe weather phenomena, simply don't have the structural strength to withstand the full onslaught of these conditions. This may be the case even though the homes have thus far survived for many years. (They may simply have never been in the direct path of the hazard.)

In other cases, some newer homes were thrown up matchbox fashion by builders who simply didn't care about how good the construction was. Sometimes this shoddy construction was not discovered (or on rare cases was allowed) by local building departments. Thus, it is possible to find even newer buildings that simply cannot handle what nature might throw at them in their area.

Which brings up the issue of how well secured a home is against whatever is likely to batter it. For our example, let's take earthquakes on the West Coast.

Modern construction involves all types of techniques to make a home earthquake proof. ("Earthquake-proof" is a misnomer, for the best that can be done is to provide additional protection—in a very big tremor, no building is likely to survive.) Some of these techniques include a deep cement foundation with bolts securing the house framing to the cement. Another technique is diagonal bracing in the walls to prevent a house from falling over in a quake. Yet another technique is to bolt the top plate (which runs around the top of the house just below the roof) and bolt the roof itself by steel rods directly down to the foundation.

All of these techniques (and others) work well in protecting a home against the dangers of an earthquake. However, not all are required of new construction. (Securing the roof and top plate to the foundation with metal, for example, is seldom if ever required by a building department.) And older construction seldom had any of these features incorporated into it.

This presents yet another environmental problem when buying a home. Perhaps a specific example will help.

In 1959, California experienced the Loma Prieta earthquake. Although the epicenter was many miles from San Francisco, that city experienced some severe problems. The most dramatic (seen widely over television) was the collapse of a portion of the Bay Bridge and some damage to what was then called "Candlestick Park."

But what was not so widely reported was the damage to homes in several areas of San Francisco. These neighborhoods used the old mudsill method noted previously and many of them slipped off their foundations and were ruined. Many were beyond salvage and had to be destroyed.

The result of this, however, for those many more buildings that weren't so severely damaged (or not even damaged at all) was that buyers began to insist on earthquake retrofitting as a condition of purchase. In other words, sellers had difficulty in disposing of the property until they had paid many thousands of dollars to have their homes secured to the foundation (and in some cases, a new foundation built).

Consider the plight of a buyer who purchased a home, say, a year before the earthquake, never thinking of asking the seller about retrofitting. Then the quake hit and even though the property itself may have sustained no damage whatever, when the owner decided to sell, there was a problem. Buyers were concerned about retrofitting . . . and wanted the seller to pay. Never mind that the seller had only been in the property a short time. Never mind that the house might be 80 years old. It's the current buyer's thinking that prevails and the current owner who has to pay.

You potentially face the same problem anytime you buy a home in an area subject to natural disasters such as earthquakes or hurricanes. Even though the house may have been standing for a long time, even though there's been no natural calamity in recent memory, that doesn't mean that something couldn't happen just the day after you buy. And then you could be caught for the costs of retrofitting, which would definitely damage your bottom line and even cause you a financial loss on reselling.

Is There Some Other Toxic Hazard?

We've only covered a few items here. There are many more, depending on your part of the country. Flooding, for example, is a common problem in the Midwest and in other areas. Some homes are on plains that may flood only once every 50 or 100 years. But when they do, the house can be under six feet or more of water.

All of which is to say that as part of your investigation when buying a home, you should endeavor to determine what problems are common to your area. Very often, real estate agents will be aware of these and to protect themselves will disclose them to you. Similarly, the seller may routinely disclose these problems. On the other hand, people tend to have short memories and if there hasn't been a problem in the area for a few decades, it may be overlooked and not mentioned.

However, a quick check with a local newspaper, the building department, or even the historical society should reveal any possible hazards. And now you can deal with them before you buy, rather than later when you want to resell and another buyer is demanding you spend money to protect against the problem.

Would You Downplay the Hazard?

I currently own a home that is only about 30 miles from an active volcano. No, it hasn't blown up in nearly a hundred years and there aren't even any old timers around who can remember the last eruption. (There are only a few photographs of it and those are mostly in museums.) But I know that in geologic terms, a hundred years is like a blink of an eye to us. It could happen again tomorrow. And suddenly the value of a home would be greatly diminished. I downplay the problem as does everyone else in the area. But how well do you think we could downplay it to a buyer if there was even the hint of another eruption?

In other words, don't downplay the threat of a potential hazard in your area. Find out what those hazards are and make every attempt to deal with them *before* you make your purchase. The last time you want to find out you have a problem, here, is when you go to resell.

Checklist for the Toxic Home

❏   Has the home been checked for radon gas?

❏   Has the gas been eliminated?

❏   Are there devices in place to prevent its return?

❏   Have you been given a lead paint disclosure?

❏   Have you read the disclosure carefully?

❏   Has the home been checked for lead paint?

❏   Will you pay for a lead paint check?

❏   Will the seller pay to have the lead paint removed?

❏   Will you?

❏   Are you satisfied to live in a home with lead paint?

❏   Has the home been checked for asbestos ceilings?

❏   What about asbestos elsewhere?

❏   Has the home been retrofitted for earthquake protection?

❏   Has the home been retrofitted for hurricane protection?

❏   Has the home been checked for other toxic elements?

There is no minimum or maximum number of checks here. You have to decide the level of concern with which you'll be willing to live.

CHAPTER 7

Buy Bigger or Smaller?

What is the optimum size for a home?

Will a bigger home resell better? Will a smaller one? At one time answers to these questions were fairly easy to guess. During the 1950s, 1960s, and 1970s, America was growing up. It was the generation of the baby boomers. Everyone had children.

And lots of kids meant the need for lots of room. Thus, if you wanted to buy a home for easy resale later on, all you had to do was to purchase as big a house as possible and you wouldn't go wrong. Bigger was definitely better.

With the end of the 1980s and the start of the 1990s, however, the baby boomers have aged and after the year 2000, many of them will be retiring. Suddenly, the big glut of large families will be gone. In its place we'll have many older people who are living just one or two to a home. Then smaller homes will be coming into vogue.

Does that mean that to be sure of a quicker resale you should now automatically look for a smaller house?

Not necessarily. It just means that you have to spend a little time assessing what age the likely buyers of your home are going to be.

In Chapter 4 we briefly discussed matching the size of your home to the likely intended buyers. For example, in a retirement area you're generally better off buying a smaller home. In a brand new tract, a bigger home is probably in order. Often, however, the choices are not so simple. With the exception of designated retirement communities, how do you know the likely age of your future buyer? Will older couples want your home? Or will younger families?

You can always take the scientific approach. If you have a nearby college or university, contact the business department. Explain that you are interested in the demographics of your area by neighborhood, if they are available. What you want to know are the trends—which areas are aging, which are seeing younger families move in.

Sometimes real estate boards and agents can be other sources and will have this information. Another option is a local newspaper or library. What's important, however, is that if you live in a major metropolitan area (and sometimes even in rural areas), chances are someone has conducted a demographic study. Check it out.

What Are You Looking For?

You are looking for trends. You want to see the average family size that's moving into the area in which you are considering buying. You want to know how long the trend has been going on and for how long it's predicted to continue.

Beware of assumptions. Don't just assume that the population in general is aging, therefore smaller houses are hot. In some areas, particularly those with high immigration, larger houses are in strong demand and that's likely to continue.

Once you get a feeling for the demographics of your area, try to match that up with your own needs. For example, if you're retired, then seek an area where many retirees are settling. Chances are you'll find a house you like there anyway, and will later on be able to resell easily for a profit.

If you're young and with a growing family, look for growth areas. You'll probably want a bigger home anyway that also may be more easy to resell later on. Remember, just avoid buying the wrong sized home for the area.

How Big Is Big, How Small Is Small?

Is 1,500 square feet big? Two thousand square feet? Three thousand square feet?

The universal measuring gauge for a home is its square footage. That's how builders determine size. That's how lenders determine size. And that, whether we like it or not, is how we must determine home size.

What's wrong with using square footage as a measurement of home size? A few years ago I owned a six-bedroom, four-bathroom house. It was seemingly huge.

Yet, it was only about 2,400 square feet. By square footage, it was relatively small. The house contained all those bedrooms and bathrooms by having smaller living, dining, and family rooms. While the house was big in the number of rooms, it was relatively small in terms of square footage.

In other words, square footage doesn't always tell the whole story. Sometimes, in fact, it works the other way. I also once owned a much smaller home in Phoenix, Arizona. The house had a darling design with a lot of mirrors in the rooms to make them look bigger. The trouble was that it was only about 1,200 square feet, with three bedrooms and two baths.

The house looked fine when you walked through it, but by living in it you quickly discovered that there just wasn't enough room. It was an uncomfortable place and because of the small size, when I sold it I did not get as much price appreciation as I had hoped to.

Although square footage is the yardstick that everyone in the industry uses, sometimes it works to your advantage and sometimes against it. But on average, it's a pretty good way of determining the size of a home.

We'll use square footage as the gauge in this chapter. But remember that sometimes the great layout of a home can more than offset the small amount of square footage. And sometimes it can't!

How Many Square Feet Should a House Have?

To get a feeling for "big" and "small" homes, let's consider the size of a "typical" home.

Few people today remember that back in the 1950s and 1960s, the typical tract home was between 1,000 and 1,200 square feet. And that accommodated three bedrooms and two baths. Custom homes that were considered very large at the time were being built with around 2,000 square feet.

Of course, as noted previously, since then we have had the impact of the baby boomers and home sizes have gone up. Today, if you talk with builders, you'll quickly discover that the average tract house is closer to 1,500 square feet, perhaps a bit larger (still three bedrooms and two baths). But custom homes are built as big as 3,500 to 5,000 square feet and more. (Back in the 1950s, 5,000 square feet used to be the size of a typical tract lot!) Obviously, our concept of what is a big house and what is a small one have both gotten bigger.

If I had to guess, I'd say that today (and probably for the next decade) any home under 1,500 square feet is going to be considered smaller (that includes condos and co-ops). Any home bigger than 1,500 square feet is going to be considered larger. Here's a quick-look chart to give you a sense for the big/ small of square footage.

Big/Small Chart

Square Footage	Type of Building
Under 1,000	Apartments, very small condos/co-ops
1,000 to 1,250	Larger apartments, smaller condos/co-ops
1,250 to 1,500	Large apartments, typical condos/co-ops, smaller houses
1,500 to 2,000	Typical houses, larger condos/co-ops
2,000 to 3,000	Larger houses, super-large condos/co-ops
More than 3,000	Superlarge house

Matching Home Size to Buyers' Needs

Remember, our goal is not just to find a house that you will want to live in. It's to look at property from an investment perspective to find a home that you will be able to resell, quickly and for a profit, a few years down the road. To repeat, that means matching the home's size to the likely buyers.

If you did your homework from the beginning of this chapter, you should have a fairly good idea of the type of family you're likely to find as a buyer for the neighborhood you are now considering. Because there are often many different-sized homes in any given neighborhood, the question becomes, what is the size that will most likely fit the most likely buyers?

What Size Home Will Larger Families Be Looking For?

Here, bigger is still better.

However, unlike in previous decades, there are many restraints on size. A bigger home costs more to heat and cool. It requires more maintenance. And, frequently, it costs more.

Therefore, although families prefer larger homes, most are resigned to the fact that they probably won't be able to get just what they want. They might like six bedrooms, but they will settle for four. They might want four bathrooms, but they might settle for two.

If you determine that the area in which you are considering the purchase of your next home is likely to be an area in which the most plentiful buyers will be families, my suggestion is that you look at a home of around 2,000 square feet. This is considered a magic number by some builders. The home is usually big enough to accommodate a family, yet small enough to not require huge heating, cooling, and maintenance bills.

I also suggest you look for a configuration of four bedrooms and three bathrooms. (Yes, you can get by with two baths, but if there are five or six in a family, it can be rather inconvenient.)

When it comes time to resell, you should have excellent luck finding a family who will be delighted to take over your home. Furthermore, because you didn't buy a large home (3,000 square feet, for example), you didn't pay a huge amount and still can resell at a reasonable price. All of which means that many families should be able to afford to buy the home you are selling.

What Size Home Will Retired People Be Looking For?

This is a relatively new phenomenon in our society—a large group of fairly well-off retired people who are frequently downsizing. They are selling off the old large family home to purchase a more modest (smaller and less expensive) (future) retirement home.

Tax laws favor those who have lived in their old large home and want to get a smaller one. As of this writing, there is a one-time $125,000 exclusion on the capital gains of a principle residence if the owner is at least 55 years old and has lived in it for three of the previous five years. (There are other conditions, so check with a tax specialist.) What this means is that an older seller does not have to pay a hefty capital gains tax when downsizing, because the tax laws are more lenient, and allow the older American to keep more of the gain on the sale.

Those who are looking at retirement usually want a smaller home. They will save on price, on taxes, on utilities, and on maintenance. But how small a home do they want?

It's not necessarily as small as you might think. Having worked with retirees for some time, I've found that many want a home large enough to accommodate family members when they come visiting. Thus, while they certainly don't want a five-bedroom home, many feel that at the very minimum, two are a necessity and three are better. Similarly, although there may be only two people in the home, two bathrooms are considered a necessity, again to some extent in anticipation for visiting children and grandchildren.

If it's a single-family house, the optimum size appears to be around 1,500 to 1,600 square feet. Typically, this means that one of the bedrooms doubles as a study or family room when not used as a bedroom. If it's a condo or co-op, 1,250 square feet will do, but usually in a configuration of two bedrooms and two bathrooms. (Usually, 1,250 square feet in three bedrooms and two baths is considered too cramped for modern living.)

Many retired people opt for condominium or co-operative living for a number of reasons. These include the fact that generally all outside areas are landscaped and maintained by a homeowners association and that often people of similar age live nearby so there's greater opportunity for social contact. Also, condos and co-ops are frequently far less expensive than buying, owning, and operating a single-family home.

What about Couples?

There is yet another phenomenon of our current age that should be addressed, if you're looking to eventually resell for a profit. I'm referring to younger couples without children. Typically, these are professionals who for one reason or another simply choose not to have children. They may be same-sex couples. They may be middle-aged and still working.

The point is that these couples are frequently looking for something different in a house and many builders are providing it for them. If you are in an area where couples without children are more a rule than an exception, you would be wise to go along with what would please them as buyers.

Generally, couples without children are looking for a different kind of home. They want a very large master bedroom and bath, large entertaining areas (living room and family room), an office area (usually doubling as a den), a well-designed food preparation area (many are gourmets), and one other bedroom for guests. Thus, the home often has only two bedrooms, but each is often a master suite with its own bath. (This also works very well for a shared home, in which two unrelated people share the expense of homeownership.)

These couples' homes are often very attractive in design, because much of the space otherwise used for extra bedrooms can be used to make two master bedroom suites. Keep in mind, however, that this is not the sort of home that a family would want under any circumstances. Thus, if you're in an area where buyers are primarily families, avoid this type of design like the plague!

Typically, this couple's home is 2,000 square feet, sometimes larger. It is most often found in urban areas and is many times seen in town houses (a form of condominium) and co-ops.

Who Is the Future Buyer of Your Home?

As we've seen in this chapter, the size of the home is important. However, the size is relevant only as it relates to the type of buyers you are likely to run into several years down the road when it comes time to resell. Thus, if you're going to be a wise buyer, you're going to spend at least a little time trying to figure out who the likely future buyer of your home will be.

As you're looking at homes to purchase for yourself, you should pay a lot of attention to the other buyers who are coming by. At an open house, for example, you will frequently see others coming through looking at the same time as you. Are they older couples? Are they younger couples without children? Are they families?

Also, ask your agent for information on the types of buyers he or she is most often dealing with. Remember, agents are specific to a local area. Thus, your agent may have some good clues here. But remember, there's always a chance your agent may not be typical or may not run into the typical buyers.

In short, try to do what police sketch artists do. Imagine in your mind's eye the future buyers of the home you are now considering purchasing. These are the people who you will have to resell to.

Do they look a lot like you? If not, maybe you're getting the wrong house. Or if it's the right house for future buyers, will you like it yourself? It's something important to consider. This is a checkslist with the future in mind. You want to find a home that fits your size requirements but will be resalable.

*C*hecklist for Bigger or Smaller

❏   Do you want a big home?

❏   Do you want a small home?

❏   Do you want a double master-suite home?

❏   Have you determined your optimum square footage?

❏   Are you within the range of size that your location will bear?

❏   Will you be satisfied in a smaller condo/townhouse?

❏   Do you know the size of the most popular resale homes in your area?

CHAPTER 8

Buy a Brand-New or Existing Home?

Here's a question that nearly all homebuyers worry over: should we buy a brand-new house or should we opt for a resale?

Most often the answer is determined by the consumer preferences of you, the buyer. Those who like tree-lined streets with lots of foliage and the look of an established neighborhood usually go for a resale. Those who prefer clean and up-to-date homes undoubtedly look for new. However, as we've seen, a decision based on consumerism may not be a wise investment in terms of future resale.

In this chapter we're going to look at the pros and cons of buying new versus resale strictly in terms of your ability to resell later on quickly and for a profit. You may be surprised at some of the conclusions.

What Are the Pros and Cons of Buying a Resale?

Each year roughly three million "secondhand" homes are sold. These range in age from only a few months to 80 years or more. What they all have in common is that they are not brand new.

Most resales are at least five years old. Five years is about the time that original buyers will be moving on. (There is a big exception and that is the resales of almost-new homes by original buyers who discovered they couldn't afford the payments. These begin happening nearly as soon as the new homes get sold.)

The biggest advantage of a resale is that it is in an established neighborhood and has a track record. An established neighborhood normally means that the trees planted when the property was brand new have grown up and are now tall and leafy. There are lots of bushes and usually the lawns are deep and green. In other words, when you drive down the street, the place just looks good.

Additionally, the homes may have styles (particularly in older neighborhoods) that many buyers find quaint and for that reason, attractive. In a way, buying in an older neighborhood is like going back in history.

Finally, established neighborhoods have a track record in terms of resale values. Sometimes it is even possible to find out what the very house you are considering sold for when brand new and then resold for many times until the present. Almost certainly you can get accurate information on recent resales in the neighborhood. And very frequently this information is available going back five years and more. In this sense, buying a resale is like a car model that's been out for a long time—you can find out up front just how well it holds its value. In the case of the home, how well it has appreciated.

On the other hand, there are definite drawbacks to resales. Many of these have to do with obsolescence and repairs. Older homes, even those only 10 or 15 years old, often do not have modern types of appliances and fixtures. Instead, they tend to be old-fashioned. This is particularly true in the use of wood colors (which seem to vary in popularity between light and dark every other decade or so), color of tile, choice of countertops, design of cabinets, and on and on. It's not so much that older homes may be in bad shape. It's that they may be simply out of fashion.

In much older homes, the number of bedrooms and baths is often too few. The design of the home may also be inadequate (kitchen too small, no family room, no den, etc.).

And as you walk down the tree-lined street, the sidewalk may have bumps in it (from tree roots lifting it up), and the street itself may need repaving or may be too narrow for modern usage.

Furthermore, as the house gets older, many of its systems need repair or replacement. This is particularly the case with roofs, heating, cooling, and plumbing. Roofs often need to be replaced by the 20th year, heating and cooling systems before the 15th year, and plumbing in houses that are 30 to 40 years old and older.

The problem is who pays for these repairs? If you buy an older home at just the right time, the previous seller gets caught for the money. But if you buy and the system breaks down or wears out during your tenure of ownership, you and you alone are probably stuck with the cost.

Having to spend a lot of money on a property is no way to make a profit later on when you sell. For example, if you buy a 15-year-old house and keep it for seven years, you might need to put in a new water heater, a new roof, a new furnace, and a new air conditioner. This could easily amount to $20,000 or more. Now when it comes time to sell, you must get $20,000 more than you otherwise would to break even. This at the same time that would-be buyers can't really see where any of the money has gone. (A roof in good repair, working plumbing, heating, and air-conditioning are assumed normal by buyers, not something they should pay extra for.) Thus, the older house can be a money pit, if you're not careful.

In conclusion, older homes are not without their problems. They have many. They also, as we've seen, have lots of pluses.

What Are the Pros and Cons of Buying New?

My wife always says, "There's nothing as nice as a brand new home!"

All the walls and ceilings are freshly painted. The flooring is new. No one has previously gotten grease on the stove, the toilets work (presumably), the shower and tub aren't yellowed, and the driveway's not oil-stained. It's like a new car—it's all yours to enjoy.

Many people agree. About a million new homes are purchased in the United States every year. And most of those buyers like the fact that their house are brand new.

There are other advantages as well. Assuming that the house was well built with good equipment, there should be no repair problems normally in the first five to seven years. You don't have to worry about fighting the garbage disposal or fixing a leaky faucet. Everything works. This is an enormous plus for all buyers, including those who will purchase from you, if you sell early on.

Furthermore, the location of the home may be closer to freeways and to train stations than older developments are. The streets are usually wider and the pavement and sidewalks are not cracked. And there's a kind of community atmosphere that comes from everyone buying at roughly the same time (being in the same boat, so to speak). Often new-home developments have friendly homeowners associations and meetings and everyone, more or less, gets to know everyone else.

That's the upside. The downside has to do with the extra costs involved initially with new homeownership. These can be many and often are not recoverable when you resell. They include:

- Installing fences

- Putting in lawns and landscaping

- Buying and installing a mailbox

- Upgrading carpeting, tile, countertops, mirror walls, closet doors, cabinets, and so on

A lot more expenses are associated with starting up a brand-new home than simply coming up with the down payment and closing costs. And these other expenses can be substantial. For this reason, many new-home buyers procrastinate in doing this work. As a result, it is not unusual to see a new tract in various stages of development for several years. A few owners have put in fences and landscaping, a few others haven't even started, and most are in between. (It is for this reason that many developers have begun including fences and at least minimal front landscaping in the cost.)

---

*N*ote

Sometimes new-home buyers have the option of paying extra for a better lot—one with a view, one that's bigger or one that's in some way better situated. Review Chapter 4 for clues on which type of lot to pay more for. If you do pay extra and it is a better lot, you'll more than get your money back when you resell. On the other hand, if you pay extra for a corner lot or a key lot or some other less desirable lot (which is possible), it's worse than wasting money, it's actually paying more for a negative.

Thus, if you buy a new home, you can expect to pay much, much more for the added features you probably will want (and will need when it comes time to resell). This increases your cost and makes turning a profit all the more difficult.

Furthermore, new homes these days typically cost more than homes of similar size in similar but established areas. The reason is the cost of construction and the cost of land (plus developing the land such as putting in sidewalks, streets, driveways, sewers, utilities, and so on).

Finally, there is the matter of a lack of track record. Will the new development perk up with later resale buyers coming in and paying even higher costs for the homes? Or will future buyers shy away, instead opting for the less expensive (by comparison) older neighborhoods? There aren't any statistics that can help here. You can't go to your local broker and get facts and figures. As a result, it's very hard to say.

I've seen it go both ways. A lot depends on the other factors discussed in Chapter 4 with regard to location. If the new development is in a choice location, almost certainly it will do well. The trouble is that most new developments must be built at the very edge of growth for the developer to get reasonable land prices (as well as enough land) for the project to succeed. Thus, unless the developer has planned wisely and the project is in the path of growth, price could stagnate. Once again, you need to spend some time doing your homework to see which way the community is growing before you buy a brand-new house.

Should You Buy Old or New?

Thus, we come back to the original question. Of course, you'll have to decide for yourself. But for me, I've almost always bought the resale.

The reason has to do more with established values than anything else. If I can find an older neighborhood (but not too old as we've seen in the last chapter) where the price has been going up steadily 5 percent or so every year, I'll take that every time over the riskiness of a brand-new tract. Of course, as noted in Chapter 4, I'll check the competition and other factors to be sure that the neighborhood isn't about ready to decline. But barring a new housing tract coming in a short distance away, for me the deciding factor is track record. The established neighborhood has it, the new one doesn't.

But is track record always that important?

I can vividly remember a number of years ago in Phoenix going from new tract of homes to new tract, checking out properties. Phoenix is unique because it has enormous amounts of land available for development. As a result, the city is an enormous sprawl in every direction. (This is not to knock

Phoenix—it's a wonderful place and I plan to buy another home there soon. It's just that it is growing almost too rapidly.)

What was most outstanding about these new tracts was that some were successful, but very many weren't. Some had the landscaping mostly in and were already becoming established neighborhoods, while others had more foreclosures and vacant homes up for resale than new ones, and this in a brand-new tract!

Was there a way to tell at the beginning which new housing tract would be successful and which wouldn't? Well, you could try the things already suggested here: check out the direction of growth and be sure that the prices were reasonable and the designs were popular. But even so, many areas that I thought should have done well, hadn't. And a few surprised me by doing well when I thought they shouldn't. In short, you just can't always predict how a new development will do.

On the other hand, you should always be able to determine exactly how well an established older neighborhood is doing.

Remember track record. It makes an enormous difference when buying a home for future resale.

How Critical Is the Age of the Property?

If you do, in fact, decide to buy an older home, the next logical question is, "How old a home should you buy?"

We've already talked about some of the major and costly problems that hit homes that are 15 to 20 years old. Even small problems begin attacking homes after they are about seven to nine years old.

In short, unless the house is under seven years of age, you can expect to have some repair and maintenance problems during your term of ownership. (This is the reason that many investors prefer properties that are three to five years old—they've had time to establish a track record, but they are not so old that they need costly work.)

If a property is beyond about seven years, my feeling is that you need to conduct a thorough inspection of the property before you make a purchase. Home inspections are common these days. But my suggestion is that you go far beyond what the typical home inspection involves.

What Is an Investor's Home Inspection?

An investor not only asks if everything in the house is working, but she also asks how long before anything needs replacement. Typically, investors have a time line in mind and they want to know if something's going to break while they own it, or after they resell it. If the time line they have in mind is three to five years and an inspection reveals that the roof has only about five years left, the wise investor usually will pass (unless it's an otherwise extraordinarily good deal). The investor knows that the replacement of the roof (which may have a life span of perhaps 25 years) will occur during her three- to five-year term of ownership and she will have to pay all the costs to resell. It doesn't make financial sense.

The same holds true for the other major systems of the house, including heating, cooling, and plumbing. (Electrical is rarely a problem unless the house is very old, as we'll see shortly.) These systems cost big bucks to replace and the next buyer never sees where the money went (and is, therefore, unwilling to pay anything extra).

What about Very Old Houses?

Houses more than 50 years old have a charm all their own. They are from a different era and often have features, such as real hardwood floors, doors, molding, railings, and so forth, that modern houses in the same price range simply could never have. Many people like the older styling and configurations.

Keep in mind, however, that an old house will have many old systems. Often the much older house was plumbed with galvanized steel pipes. When these pipes are between 30 and 50 years of age (sometimes sooner), they have a tendency to rust out. Replacing them with copper plumbing can be very expensive. Old electrical systems often don't carry a separate ground wire, something considered essential for safety in modern homes. Rewiring is likewise expensive. Many older homes may have, for example, gravity-feed furnaces. These are noisy and usually are replaced by a modern heating system when they stop working—again very expensive. And, of course, there are all the old-style and sometimes not-working fixtures in the bathrooms and kitchen (not to mention enlarging and creating new bathrooms).

In short, the very old house can be nothing more than a money pit. If, however, it's in a great neighborhood where there is no longer any room to build new houses and where sales indicate a strong buyer demand over the years, it still may be worthwhile to buy one.

I can recall looking at one of these older homes in a very highly desired neighborhood near Oakland, California. The floor was partly rotted out by termites. The water heater was an old copper-tube type not used in 50 years (impossible to fix). The heating system was virtually nonexistent. The electrical system needed complete renovation. The roof leaked. My own estimate was that it would take a minimum of $35,000 just to put the property back into livable condition, and no one would ever see where the money went.

Yet, the owner received five offers on it the day that the house was put on the market, one of them for more than the full asking price! Why? The neighborhood had a wonderful track record. Homes there always appreciated in value. Buyers knew that no matter what, they would always be able to resell later on for a profit.

Buy old or new? In my opinion it's less risky to buy old. But you can do very well buying well-located new homes. To shave the odds against you either way, do your homework: find the direction of growth and check the track record.

---

*C*hecklist for a Brand-New or Existing Home

- ❑   Is the resale home in a good, established neighborhood?
- ❑   Does the neighborhood have a good price gain track record?
- ❑   Are there enough bedrooms and bathrooms in the resale? Is the resale obsolete or in disrepair?
- ❑   Is the brand-new home well located?
- ❑   Is it well built?
- ❑   Does it come with a sound warranty?
- ❑   Are you prepared for incidentals (like fences and upgrades)?
- ❑   Does the brand-new home's price compare well with existing homes?
- ❑   Is the entire new home tract built up already?
- ❑   Are you avoiding buying "on spec," sight unseen?
- ❑   Have you conducted an "investor's" home inspection?
- ❑   Are you wary of very old homes?

Lots of checks suggest you're doing your homework when it comes to comparing old and new. Few checks are worrisome and may indicate you haven't thought the age problem all the way through.

CHAPTER 9

How to Check Out the Market

When is the right time to buy your next home?

For most people, the right time to buy is when they have enough money for the down payment and enough income to handle the mortgage. Or it's when they've had a job change demanding that they move into a new area. Or when they outgrow their old home either because they now have children and the house too small, or because the children have grown up and left and now the house is too big.

You get the idea. For most people, buying a new home comes about because their situation dictates it. In fact, making the decision itself tends to be a very personal thing. Most people don't consult with anybody outside of their immediate family. It's kind of like the decision to buy a car . . . or maybe a refrigerator. It's a consumer decision.

But as we've already seen, buying a home is too costly a proposition to regard strictly with consumer eyes. Do that and your biggest purchase in a lifetime might end up being your biggest loss in a lifetime.

It's important to consider the home purchase in terms of investment. For how much profit can you eventually resell has to be the biggest question.

Unfortunately, when you're ready to buy and when it's right to buy can be two totally different times. Just because you have the cash for the down payment, the income to handle the monthly payments and the desire and need to move isn't enough, not from an investment perspective. The market has to be right, as well.

Are There Market Cycles?

It wasn't that long ago when most people felt that real estate was the only field in which prices went up and up. From the beginning of World War II until about 1989, that was a truism. You could throw cash at almost any piece of real estate virtually anywhere in the country and count on the fact that when you went to resell, you'd get more than you originally paid. Anytime used to be the right time to buy.

That up cycle lasted a long while, almost 50 years. Enough time for the generation that saw the Great Depression and the effects it had on real estate to pass on, leaving a younger generation that had never seen anything but good times, at least in terms of property. How many people now living (and more importantly involved in a home purchase decision) can recall that property values across the country fell by something like 60 percent or more during the early 1930s? How many can recall the enormous number of people who were dispossessed of their homes through foreclosure during that time?

What we don't see we tend to ignore. On the other hand, most of us do believe what we see. As a result, after 50 years of consistent real estate growth, most people just couldn't or just wouldn't believe anything bad about property values.

The reality, however, is that real estate is not much different from stocks, bonds, and commodities. There are periods of time when prices are rising—and also time periods when they are falling. Beginning roughly in 1989, after a spurt in price appreciation, real estate turned down and remained down in many areas of the country well into the 1990s. No, it wasn't the Great Depression all over again. But if you were one of those who was trying to resell and was told your mortgage was higher than the reduced value of your home, it may have felt the same.

The decade of the 1990s, at least the early years, proved that home prices can go down as well as up.

The Consequences of Buying into a Down Market

It's easy to speak of not buying when prices are falling. If a house is worth $100,000 and it looks like (based on market conditions) it's going to be worth $95,000 in six months, you would be well advised to stay away and not purchase it. (We'll discuss buying options in a down market shortly.)

Holding off on a purchase may be the soundest financial course when the market is falling. Even though your wallet's ready and you're all psyched up to move, holding off may save— indeed make—you more money than buying.

Holding back may be hard to do, but the need to follow this tactic in a falling market should be fairly obvious. What's not so obvious, however, is that buying just before the top of a cycle can be even more disastrous than buying on the way down. In other words, if you buy at or near the peak of the market, you're going to lose and lose big.

The legion of those who fall into this camp is enormous. Literally millions of buyers purchased homes at the very end of the 1980s at very inflated prices. Then, when the market turned, virtually overnight they saw losses of 25 percent and more. It's a sobering thought.

Some simply held on (and are still holding on), waiting for prices to come back up. Others sold at a loss. Still others found that they had to move and couldn't sell and, thus, found themselves in foreclosure (where they lost not only their home but their credit as well).

Is There a Strategy for Success?

When it comes to market timing, the only strategy that makes sense is this:

Buy Near the End of the Down Cycle and the Beginning to the Middle of the Up Cycle

If you buy near the bottom, you may encounter a loss for a short time. But as soon as the market turns around, you'll benefit from appreciating prices. Similarly, if you buy at the beginning to the middle of the upward cycle, you will similarly benefit as prices continue to inflate. You tend to lose if you buy at or near the peak or on the way down.

It's important to understand that we're now speaking of an influence on price that is totally removed from the value a home gets from being in a good location, from being fixed up, from the seller offering good terms, and so on. All of these help. But if during your tenure of ownership prices of homes in general go down, then your house's value will go down as well, no matter what you do.

On the other hand, if the rate of home appreciation in your area is only 5 percent a year (which it was on average for many, many years), at the end of five years your house will be worth 25 percent more than you paid for it (not counting compounding that would make it worth much more), all other factors aside. In a situation like this you don't have to be clever or do anything special—just be sure you are ready to sell your home in the same condition that you bought it in and you'll do ok.

In short, watch out for market cycles—they can make you . . . or break you.

How Do I Know Where the Market Is?

This, of course, is the real question. How do you know whether the market is currently going up or going down? More importantly, how do you recognize where you are on the cycle—at the beginning, middle, or end of a swing?

We'll see how to determine this shortly, but first you must remember that historically upswings tend to last a long time, while downswings last a much shorter time. Following is a chart that shows the real estate market in the United States since the turn of the past century. (Dates are approximations because the market moves at a somewhat different pace in different areas of the country. The last downtrend in your area, for example, could have started in 1988 or 1990, even though the date given here says 1989.)

100-Year Cycle for Home Price Appreciation

1995 to Current	Upswing
1989 to 1995	Downswing
1941 to 1988	Upswing[*]
1930 to 1940	Downswing[**]
1915 to 1929	Upswing
1897 to 1914	Downswing

[*]During this long period there were numerous times when prices remained static for a few years, for example, in the mid-1950s. This is not the same as a downswing. Rather, it meant that if you bought in 1957 and you went to sell in 1959, you might not get much more for your house than you paid for it. If you waited only a few more years, however, you would receive significantly more.

[**]Housing prices actually stabilized around 1936 and began to move upward into 1937, but then prices collapsed again until the beginning of World War II.

An important point to glean from this historical chart is to recognize that upswings, generally, last longer than downswings. This means that if the market is going down and you must wait to buy, you won't have to wait long. Chances are the turnaround will come within five to seven years. On the other hand, if the market's going up, your chances of riding with it are excellent for it may continue its upswing for a much longer period of time.

Isn't It Easy to Tell Where You Are in the Cycle?

It's not always so simple as it sounds to know where the real estate market is at any given time. I can recall that in the summer of 1989 a friend was selling a home in Southern California. That was the very peak of the market. In July, prices were going up. By August, they had peaked and started down. His sale didn't occur until October. The price he had to accept, because of the market reversal, was roughly 10 percent less than the highest price a similar house had sold for only a few months earlier. If only he had known that the bubble on rising prices was going to burst, he could have sold months earlier and made much more profit. (He didn't quibble, however, because he was still making nearly a 100 percent profit from having bought right in the first place.)

On the other hand, consider the plight of those people who bought right at the top of the market in July. Within months they saw the value (if they sold) of their property dropping 10 percent. If they put up a typical 20 percent down payment, that amounted to an erasure of half their equity. I'm sure that was a sobering experience!

Can You Refine Your Timing?

Could my friend have studied a little to discover just when the market would peak and have sold before? Could a buyer have conducted the same research and bought just after?

Probably not. When I say the market peaked in August of that year, I do that with the full knowledge that comes from hindsight. At the time, I don't think anyone realized what was happening. The first warning that most agents got was when the number of sales suddenly fell. The next was when sellers were forced to drop prices to sell their properties.

In short, it's very hard to know when you're at the peak of the market, at the moment. A year later looking back it's very easy to see. But there, at the time? It would take someone with the wisdom of Solomon and the foresight of Nostradamus to figure it out.

The same holds true for bottoms. Again I was in Southern California at the bottom of the past cycle. But it was very difficult to discern where that bottom was. Much of the country's real estate had recovered by 1994. Even in 1996, however, the Southern California market was still spotty, still bouncing along the bottom.

How Do I Find Out about the Market?

The fact that it's confusing to know where the real estate market is at a particular time means that a little research is in order. After all, if you can get a handle on where the market is and act on that information, you can almost guarantee to have an easy time reselling later for a profit.

Ask Agents

Ask any agent. Or better, ask a half dozen agents. Their livelihoods depend on commissions and they only get a commission when they sell a property. If they're selling a lot of houses (an up market), they're going to be very happy and upbeat. If they can't make a sale for love or money, they will be very downbeat.

---

*N*ote

This goes beyond just asking about the price differences in an area over a period of time as suggested in Chapters 2 and 4. Here we are trying to determine an overall sense of where the market is, not the best location within a given market.

The reason I suggest asking several agents, rather than just one, is that selling real estate is a fairly difficult profession to be in and a surprisingly large number of agents rarely sell much property in any market, good or bad. They are likely to tell you the market's down no matter when you ask!

Another drawback to asking an agent is the fact that buyers always want to make low offers and sellers always ask high prices. Therefore, as a defense, many agents automatically suggest to both buyers and sellers that the market looks bleak. This tends to keep selling prices and offers more reasonable.

Check the News Media

Housing is an important part of virtually every local economy. Furthermore, many people consider their equity as their nest egg, their largest asset, and as a consequence are always curious about what housing prices are doing.

It's only natural, therefore, that local newspapers and magazines will spend a lot of time focusing on the housing market. If you're new to an area, the first thing you should do (even before stopping at a real estate office or scouting out neighborhoods) is to subscribe to the local newspaper or magazine (if there is one). Just by reading the news, over the course of a month, you should begin to get an excellent feel for how the market is in the area. Many times newspapers and magazines will even include detailed charts by area and over time show how prices have gone up or down. In any event, if it's a down market, you can be sure they'll be lamenting the fact. And if it's an up market, they work just as hard to report on it.

Talk with Lenders

Lenders have their pulse on the market. After all, no one (ok, almost no one) pays cash for a home. Instead, we all take out a mortgage. If we're late on payments or, worse, don't make them, the lenders know. As a result, lenders know intimately how the market is doing, sometimes better than the agents do.

However, there are true lenders and there are retailers. A true lender is typically a bank or a savings and loan that actually puts up money. A retailer is a mortgage broker. While the loan officer of a bank or savings and loan will have an excellent feel for how the market is doing, a mortgage broker may only know how his volume of business is holding up. The reason is simple: the mortgage broker simply makes the loan and then forgets about it. It's up to the bank, savings and loan, and the secondary market to worry if that mortgage goes sour. The mortgage broker, as long as all the paperwork was correct, may never even hear about it.

Check It Out on the Internet

Increasingly, the Internet offers real estate information. A number of columns are run regularly from the major providers and there are sometimes local chat rooms where you can discuss the market. In addition, bulletin boards and search engines will help you turn up additional information.

In the past I would suggest going to the library and reading recent magazine articles to see how the market was doing. These days, however, such a wealth of information is available from the Internet that I think it's almost a better source. Of course, nothing is to prevent you from doing both!

Ask the County Tax Collector

Property taxes are almost universally *ad valorem* taxes. This means that they are assessed based on the market value of the property. In up markets, the taxes are rising; in down markets, taxes fall. Simply find out what's happening from the tax collector.

How Do I Locate the Exact Point of the Cycle I'm In?

As suggested previously, you probably can't. The best you can really hope to do is find out whether the market is going up or down and for how long that's been happening.

Here are some helpful suggestions, however, that may keep you from getting hurt by peaks and troughs:

Generally speaking, in real estate as in most other financial markets, including stocks, bonds, and commodities, the market accelerates just before it goes bust. In other words, real estate prices were appreciating faster in 1988, just before the market peak, then they had been in the previous five years.

The lesson to be learned here is that if you're in an up market that's been doing well for a fairly long period of time (perhaps a decade or more) and suddenly prices begin accelerating very fast, be careful. The market could be blowing out just prior to peaking.

One caveat is in order here and that's when there's high inflation. To some extent, homes are a commodity and respond to inflation like other commodities. When inflation is high, prices tend to go up. When inflation is low, prices tend to be moderate. With housing, of course, this is mitigated by the fact that the interest rates likewise tend to follow inflation. In higher inflation, we get higher interest rates, which means high-cost mortgages, cutting down on sales. Similarly in lower inflation, the interest rates on mortgages tend to drop, making it easier to find buyers who qualify and to get sales.

On the other hand, bottoms of markets tend to be kind of bumpy. Instead of simply picking a month where prices are lowest and then seeing them respond upward, at the bottom, prices tend to bounce around, up a month or two, then down a month or two. There is little clarity.

The reason for this is that when prices are declining, sellers pull houses off the market. Many sellers simply refuse to sell at this time.

As soon as it becomes general knowledge that the market is turning around, however, these people list their homes. Thus, at the bottom, new buyers may quickly purchase the existing inventory and put upward pressure on prices. As soon as prices and volume of sales increase, however, more sellers who wanted to sell but were holding off list their homes. This extra supply puts downward pressure on prices, until the existing inventory is absorbed by new buyers and the market starts off again.

The process is described aptly as "bumping along the bottom" and it continues until the inventory of both listed as well as "wannabe listed" homes is absorbed. Then prices can truly begin to rise.

Should I Really Wait if the Market Isn't Right?

The whole theme of this chapter has been that to buy right, you should never buy into a down market. That means don't buy at the peak or while the market's falling. Just wait. In a year or so you'll very likely get the house of your dreams for far less than if you bought it now. And that money you save will be money you would have otherwise lost.

Nevertheless, there's a certain frenzy that buyers of houses or cars or any other big-ticket items get into that can be expressed by the statement, "I want it, I want it now, I deserve it, and I'm going to get it!"

Just going out and looking at homes for sale can cause this frenzy to erupt. And once it's churning in your blood, it's hard to turn it off. You'll begin to say to yourself that no matter what, you've got to get a house.

If that's your situation, here's a strategy for buying right (or almost right) into a down or declining market.

How to Buy into a Down Market

To succeed in a down market, you must buy low enough that you won't get hurt if the market goes down further or the market levels out but doesn't start up soon enough for you to sell for enough profit to pay your sales costs (closing costs plus commission).

That means lowballing the seller.

When you lowball a property, you offer far, far less than the seller is asking. The seller, for example, may be asking $200,000 and you offer $150,000. That's a lowball offer.

Most sellers won't accept such an offer. They'd rather sit on the property and not sell than accept and possibly take a loss. Certainly that's the case in a market that's either swinging up or bouncing along the bottom.

But in a market that's in free fall where no one knows how low prices will go, some sellers will bite the bullet and accept lowball offers. They reason that it's better to get out now, while they can, than sit around waiting for a better buyer who may never show up.

If you want to buy in a down market, make only lowball offers. If you don't, you'll be helping the seller enormously. And you'll be digging yourself into a pit from which it may take you years and tens of thousands of dollars to escape.

And just in case you've a mind not to heed this advice, let me bring a sobering phrase to mind, "upside down." During the past downward cycle in real estate housing, a lot of people who had bought either at the peak or on the way down in no time found they owed more than the value of their property. They were upside down; their mortgage was higher than their home's value. Too often foreclosure and lost home and credit were the results.

If you don't want to be upside down, don't let a buying frenzy sway you from clearheaded thinking. If the market is bad, don't buy. Or if you do buy, get such a good deal that you can't go wrong. There's no other way to do it.

On the other hand, if the market's good, jump right in. With prices going up all around you, it's hard not to make a profit.

What Is the Next Cycle Going to be Like?

As this book is written, the next cycle, an upward swing, has been in effect for several years in most parts of the country. A few areas, such as Southern California, are still bumping along the bottom.

The real question is not when the market will turn around. It appears to have already done so. The question is how long and how steep will the upturn be?

I have no clear sense of how long this up market will last, except that because we have had a rather big fall, housing has established a fairly solid bottom from which to rise. I suspect it will carry on for some time, probably well into the next century. Factors that will determine the length include inflation, interest rates and the number of new housing units built. (A housing shortage already exists across most of the country.)

On the other hand, the steepness of the upward swing is a bit clearer. It appears that price appreciation will be modest in most areas for some time to come. This means under 5 percent, often around 1 or 2 percent.

The reason is that today's buyers have a much stronger feeling for a down market. At the beginning of this chapter we noted that buyers in the late 1980s believed prices could only go up, for they had forgotten (or never known) the problems of the Great Depression.

Today's buyers, however, have strong memories of the real estate recession of the early 1990s. Often they, their friends, or their relatives saw the price of their homes decline. Almost everyone knows somebody who had to take a licking when they sold. Many people at least have acquaintances who were upside down. Some even know those who lost their homes to foreclosure.

In other words, today, nobody seriously doubts that the residential real estate market has cycles. And most people are wary of buying a home at too high a price, lest they lose money when they sell. And this knowledge and wariness act to moderate price increases. It's simply the case that today's wise buyers are not going to get caught and so when sellers try to raise prices too fast, too far, the buyers back off.

In short, don't expect quick price appreciation (except in a few localized areas that for one reason or another are in high demand) anytime soon. More likely we're going to see a fairly stable market for years to come.

---

*C*hecklist for Market Conditions

❑   Is the current market up?

❑   Is the current market down?

❑   Is the current market in between?

❑   Are you sure?

❑   Have you asked several agents?

❑   Have you checked the news media?

❑   Have you checked with the tax collector's office?

❑   Will you buy no matter what the market conditions?

❑   Will you wait, if necessary, until times get better?

❑   Are you buying near the end of the down cycle, or start of the up?

❑   Are you prepared to "lowball" in a down market?

You need to check the questions carefully. The last thing you want to do is buy as the market collapses and end up owing more than you paid for the home!

CHAPTER 10

Always Leave a Back Door Open

It's been said many times that having a back door to a living space is a safety necessity. Whether it's an apartment, a condo, or even a hotel room, it's vital to have an alternate way out. A fire or some other unforeseen calamity could occur that could block the main entrance before you could escape. Without that back door, you would be trapped and might perish.

The same holds true from an investment perspective when buying a home. When we buy, we always have high hopes and wonderful expectations. We'll put our down payment and closing costs into the house and then be able (albeit sometimes with some strain) to make those monthly payments. We'll live there for a period of years and then, when we decide it's time to move on, we'll sell, getting all of our money out plus, hopefully, a substantial profit.

As you read through this book you'll find all types of techniques you can utilize to help make this happen. Indeed, for most people this is just how it does turn out.

But not always.

Sometimes a calamity, a financial fire so to speak, occurs and you can't get out the front door of your investment. The plans you originally made won't work. Unless you have an escape hatch, you could be facing the inability to make payments, loss of the home through foreclosure, and permanently ruined credit.

But, you may be saying to yourself, that's most unlikely. I'm a solid citizen with a good job and a nice house in a fine neighborhood. What could happen that would prevent my exiting the property gracefully with a profit, as long as I make the monthly mortgage payments? Here are some possibilities that have burned others:

- A downturn in the market could make it more difficult to sell and result in your receiving a lower price.

- Financial difficulty (loss of job, job transfer) might mean you'd want to sell far sooner than you anticipated, before the market had a chance to rise enough to allow you to acquire more equity.

- Personal problems (health crisis, divorce) might make you suddenly have to sell quickly and get out with as much cash as possible.

Or something else might occur that simply demanded that you change your plans. You had anticipated holding on to your house for a number of years, perhaps seven to nine, and now it's only been two and you have to get out. You anticipated you'd be able to list your house on the market and get a good offer, but now you're "upside down" and it will actually cost you out-of-pocket money to sell! You thought that buyers would be streaming to your house, but none can be found. The house has become a financial disaster for you, mainly because your "front door plan," how you originally anticipated you'd exit, is closed.

What do you do when your best-laid plans don't work out? How do you handle a disaster?

Like a Boy Scout, Be Prepared

The answer, of course, is to try to anticipate future problems and provide solutions for them before they occur. As we are suggesting, the idea is to structure your purchase to leave yourself a "back door" out in case of emergency.

In this chapter we're going to consider several backdoor options that you may need someday. You'll need to prepare for some of them *at the time you make your purchase.* For others, you'll just need to keep them stored in the back of your head to use as alternatives if and when disaster should strike. Here's the first.

Is Your Mortgage Assumable?

This is a true story about a close friend of mine, Susan. Susan bought a home in the Phoenix, Arizona, market a few years ago at a time when the valley was booming. Prices were accelerating upward and she felt that she would only need to stay in the place two or three years and then be able to sell for a profit.

However, as she was making her purchase and coming out of her agent's office, she happened to meet with a reporter from a Los Angeles newspaper. He was in town doing a feature story on the Phoenix market to run in their big Sunday edition. He was, in fact, looking to interview people who were buying into the booming market and Susan suddenly became a prime candidate.

She, of course, was thrilled to be interviewed and told him how lovely the house was, its excellent location, the community swimming pool, and on and on. The reporter listened, nodded, took notes, thanked her for her help, and left with the intriguing comment, "I hope this boom works out better than the last one."

Susan wasn't the type of person to let anything slide and so she caught up to the reporter and asked him exactly what he meant by "the last one."

He seemed surprised at the question, but was open with his answer. He pointed out that the Phoenix area was both blessed and cursed by an abundance of land. The valley covers hundreds of square miles and provides developers with all types of opportunities for putting up houses. In addition, there was a seemingly endless supply of water from the Colorado River to handle a burgeoning population.

As a result, the area had seen a series of booms and busts. The market would be strong and in an effort to cash in on it, too many developers would put up too many houses. The supply would outstrip the demand and for a few years there would be a real estate bust. But ever more and more people came into the valley until eventually the supply was used up and a boom period would start again. It had been going that way for some time and the reporter said, not to dampen Susan's enthusiasm, that he was hoping it wouldn't happen again for her sake.

Susan thanked him for the information and thought on it. Then she considered the deal she was making from an investment perspective. She was buying a home and putting 20 percent of her own cash down on a conventional (nongovernment-insured or guaranteed) mortgage. When she sold, the next buyer would have to do the same thing—come up with a down payment and a new mortgage to buy her out. But what if the area was in a bust period when she wanted to sell? Would she be able to find another buyer like her? Would that buyer have enough money for the down payment? Could that buyer qualify for the new mortgage?

Suddenly Susan wasn't sure anymore. She turned around, walked back into the real estate office, and backed out of her deal. (She had allowed herself ten days to approve an inspection of the property. The time limit wasn't up, and it turned out the home had some defects, so she simply said she didn't approve of the property and that was that for the deal. It's a typical contingency clause that most buyers use and some exercise to get out of making a purchase. For more information, consult my book, *Buy Your First Home,* Dearborn Financial Publishing, Inc., 1996.)

Then Susan went looking for a different kind of property, from an investor's perspective. It took her a few weeks, but eventually she found exactly what she wanted. A buyer had recently purchased a home in the same tract as Susan wanted and now was forced to sell because of a job transfer. However, the owner had bought the home using a Department of Veterans Affairs (VA) loan. (The VA guarantees mortgages to qualifying veterans allowing them to purchase with no down payment and minimum closing costs. These loans were assumable.)

The owner wanted only 10 percent down to the assumable loan. Susan quickly jumped on the deal, because there were many others who wanted it as well. She got into the property with half the down payment she had anticipated paying and now, more importantly, had an assumable loan, meaning that someone else could assume it from her, essentially without qualifying.

As it turned out, the boom/bust cycle repeated and within a year things had turned around to the point where prices were falling and it seemed like every other house was for sale. Unfortunately, it was at this very time that Susan developed a health problem and was forced to leave the area (she no longer could take the intense summer heat). She had to sell into a down market.

When she called an agent, she was told she probably couldn't get more than the amount of her mortgage, let alone what she had paid for the property. It would cost her out-of-pocket money for the commission and closing costs. She wasn't exactly upside down yet, but the way the market was falling, she soon would be.

So Susan acted quickly and decisively. She put an advertisement in the paper offering her property for sale by the owner for $1, cash, no qualifying for a new mortgage.

Yes, even in a down market, she got a lot of interest and more than a few offers. She took the best-qualified buyer and sold him the property for $1, cash. The buyer assumed her existing mortgage and also gave her a second mortgage for her equity, no payments, no interest, all due in five years.

Susan was out.

No, it wasn't a wonderful deal. She certainly wasn't thrilled about getting $1. And she was well aware that it was a gamble as to whether or not she'd ever get paid on that second mortgage.

On the other hand, she might get paid. And she certainly was out of the property. And her credit remained perfect. She had no foreclosure, no late payments, no bad credit whatsoever.

The Assumable Mortgage Back Door

What made this true story possible was the fact that Susan had an assumable mortgage on her property. She could virtually give the property to anyone else and as long as that person took over (assumed) responsibility for making the mortgage payments, she was out.

If Susan did not have an assumable mortgage, the next buyer would have to obtain a brand-new mortgage. That would have meant qualifying, putting up a down payment (most lenders do require a down payment as a condition for getting the loan) and paying closing costs for the mortgage (points and all types of fees that lenders charge). With the assumable mortgage, Susan simply paid a $50 assumption fee and that was it.

The assumable mortgage was Susan's back door. It wasn't something she planned on using. Indeed, she had hoped that her property would have appreciated in value to the point that when it was time to resell, she would get lots more money from a buyer who would simply get a much higher new loan. But when times turned tough, the assumable mortgage was there and she was able to use it to bail out.

A back door isn't like a front door—you don't use it on a regular basis. But when there's a fire and your home is burning up, it's a great way to save yourself.

Can You Get an Assumable Mortgage?

There's really only one problem with Susan's story: a buyer who puts up only $1 isn't really very interested in keeping the property financially sound. Too many of these second buyers, when times get tough for them, simply walk. The result is that the lenders end up having to foreclose and take lots of properties back. So many people have used assumable mortgages for this purpose in bust markets, and so many times lenders have been the "fall guys," that today most lenders won't make truly assumable mortgages. This means these mortgages are more difficult to come by. Not impossible, but difficult.

Older Federal Housing Administration (FHA) and VA loans, in many cases, are still fully assumable. You have to check with the lender to be sure. There are literally millions of these that remain on the books. And a seller who has one often will advertise the fact, for it's a financial plus in favor of the house.

One problem with getting an older loan, however, is that often the price of the property has increased to the point where the assumable mortgage represents only a small portion, say half, of the property's value. This means that you have to come up with the other half from some other place.

Of course, that's not always difficult. There's no reason you can't insist that the seller who has an assumable government mortgage give you an assumable second mortgage, as part of the purchase price, to go along with it. For example, the assumable first could be half of the purchase price and the assumable second could be 30 percent or 40 percent, meaning you'd put down only 10 percent or 20 percent. Yes, deals such as this are made every day.

The Assumable Second

A few years ago I was buying a property and was attempting to construct the purchase to leave myself a back door. The house had an assumable FHA mortgage on it and the value was roughly 60 percent of the purchase price. This meant I had to come up with another 40 percent, a substantial amount *if* it were to be in cash.

I proposed the following to the seller. I would come up with 5 percent cash down, assume the existing government mortgage, and the seller would give me a second mortgage for 35 percent (at a low interest rate and payments, by the way) that was "onetime assumable."

I can still remember the seller asking, "What does 'one time assumable' mean?"

I explained it meant that if I wanted to sell the property, I could let the next buyer assume that second mortgage without the seller's approval. It made the second mortgage just as assumable as the first.

The seller didn't like that at all. So I then pointed out that it could be done *only once.* That next buyer couldn't resell without paying off the second. It was assumable for only one time. I explained that it was a safety net for me, just in case something happened to me financially and I had to sell.

The seller saw my reasoning and also saw that the market wasn't wonderful at the time. The seller agreed. (As it turned out, I never had to use the back door because the market turned up and I was able to sell fine [by the front door], later on. But the escape hatch was there, should I have needed it.)

Other Assumables?

There are other assumable mortgages available, but they usually aren't fully assumable. For example, adjustable rate mortgages (at any given time representing 30 percent to 55 percent of the market) often are advertised as assumable. What that means, however, is that when you go to sell, the next buyer can assume the mortgage, provided she qualifies for it almost as if it were a brand new loan. That's not really assumable, except that the lender may charge the assuming buyer fewer (or no) points and the qualifying may not be quite so rigorous. It does make the mortgage more attractive, but the back door it gives you tends to be open only a crack. If hard times occur, maybe you can slip through . . . and maybe not.

You can also get assumables from sellers who own their property free and clear. Just as in the previous case where the seller gave me an assumable second, a seller can also give an assumable first.

How Do I Get an Assumable First Mortgage?

Indeed, it is often the case that a seller who owns property free and clear will be anxious to give a large first mortgage to a qualified buyer. Many times sellers don't want to receive a large sum in cash. They may not need it to purchase another home and now it becomes a matter of finding an investment vehicle that will pay them interest on the money. Usually, this is the case when the seller is retired and is looking to pick up extra income. The interest rate on a first mortgage is almost always going to be considerably higher than what a bank would pay for a certificate of deposit. It's guaranteed by the house (which the seller can take back if the buyer doesn't make the payments). It's a safe, steady source of income.

As a seller with a paid-off property, I wouldn't hesitate for a moment to give a qualified buyer a new first. And it's not unusual for such buyers to ask that the new first be assumable, at least "onetime," providing them with a way out—a back door.

Go for the Assumable

Assumable loans are your first line of defense. They provide an excellent escape hatch. No, it's not always possible to get both the house of your dreams and a home that has an assumable loan. But, it couldn't hurt to look. As noted in Chapter 2, what you want to do is to blend the two paths—buying as a consumer and buying as an investor. If you can come to a happy compromise by buying both a home that you like as well as one that has a back door, you'll sleep much better at night.

Why Can't I Just Walk Away?

At this point, I'm sure that some readers are wondering what the fuss is all about. After all, if things get bad, if you can't make the payments or you get upside down (on your mortgage), why not just walk away from the turkey? For many people, at least in the back of their minds, their back door is to skip town. If worse comes to worst, they'll pack up and leave the house to the mortgage company.

"Walking" is a technique that is commonly used. During the past real estate recession, hundreds of thousands of homeowners used it. Disgusted with falling prices and compelled to leave the area, they just walked away from their homes. Eventually, the lender discovered this (when the monthly payments stopped coming in), foreclosed on the homes, took possession, refurbished them and then resold them, later on to other buyers.

What's wrong with this scenario? Why won't it work as a backdoor technique?

It's important to understand that some things that look good on the surface actually can be rotten underneath. Walking away and leaving a house to the lender is one of them. If there's any message you take away from this book, it's never, *never,* walk away from a house.

I'm not saying this because I have any vested interest in lenders—I don't. My concern is with your credit and your ability to get another mortgage on another house.

If a lender forecloses on you (takes back the house because you haven't made payments), that fact goes onto your credit history and remains there for a very, very long time. Long after a bankruptcy or a divorce has been forgotten, the foreclosure remains. (I sold a house nearly 17 years ago and the new buyer assumed my existing mortgage, taking over full responsibility for it. However, in an error in documentation the title insurance company forgot to send the lender instructions to take my name off the mortgage. Subsequently, that new buyer defaulted (stopped making payments) and the house went into foreclosure. Because my name was still on the loan, that foreclosure was reported to credit reporting companies. And to this day when I apply for a new mortgage, it comes up and I have to explain it showing the documentation from that original sale. Of course, once explained, the problem goes away. But after 17 years it still comes up . . . and if there wasn't a good explanation, chances are I couldn't get a new mortgage!

Mortgage lenders are very unforgiving about mortgages. They are ready to forgive (with a reasonable explanation) late payments on your car or nonpayments on your credit card, particularly if this was a couple of years ago and you've reestablished good credit since then. But let them hear that you were late on a mortgage payment or, crime of all crimes, that you allowed a property you owned to go into foreclosure, and they never will forgive (or forget).

Thus, while walking away from a home may seem like a simple and easy solution to a difficult problem, what it actually does is destroy your future for a quick fix in the present. After a foreclosure you may find you can establish credit fairly readily for credit cards and even bank loans. But chances are you will find it very difficult if not impossible to get a new mortgage for years and years to come.

My suggestion, therefore, is to give up the thought that walking away from it is a possible back door. Nail that idea shut tight and never open it. There are other alternatives.

Can You Put Your House on the Auction Block?

Here's a technique that you can use as a back door, if you can't arrange for an assumable mortgage when you buy: the auction. It's important to understand that you don't need to exercise this when you purchase the property, except perhaps with some discretion in choosing your lender. On the other hand, if you know about it before you buy, you can keep it under your hat until you are ready to use it.

The home auction became popular during the past real estate recession when prices were so low in so many areas that the only way some sellers could attract buyers was to auction off their property. Typically, this type of sale requires an aggressive seller who's got a lot of nerve and is willing to take some risks. However, when it works, it can pay off.

If you are right side up and have some equity, then little planning is necessary to handle an auction. You simply decide when you're going to do it and attempt to pull it off. (We'll have more to say about the auction process shortly.)

Because an auction tends to be a desperate step, most people don't consider it until they are in a desperate situation; namely that they are upside down on their mortgage. Now an auction is problematic. If the buyer doesn't come up with enough money to pay off the high mortgage, the sale is moot because the lender will still foreclose against the person who took out the mortgage—you. You'll still lose your house and your credit.

Therefore, what we're going to consider here is planning ahead, creating a back door, so to speak, for using an auction when times get really tough and you are upside down.

Can I Force a Lender to Accept a Deal?

When you are upside down, it's very unlikely that anyone is going to pay you enough money for your house to pay off your mortgage. After all, your problem is that you owe more than your home is worth. Thus it doesn't matter if you list, sell by owner, or auction. The problem is you owe too much.

There are only a couple of solutions in this situation. The first is to make up the difference yourself out of your pocket. That's right, if the mortgage is $150,000 and the house is worth $130,000, you auction it off to the highest bidder (who is likely to bid $130,000 unless you get very lucky) and then you come up with the difference of $20,000 out of pocket to pay off the mortgage.

The advantage here is that you get out with your good name and good credit intact. You also lose everything you originally put into the property plus more at the resale, in this case $20,000 more.

Another solution is to force the lender to accept a "short sale" and a "short payoff." Ten years ago these terms weren't even in the real estate vernacular. Today, they are commonly used and understood by everyone in the field.

A "short sale" is where you sell the house for less than the mortgage amount. A "short payoff" is where the lender accepts less than the amount due on the mortgage and considers it paid off in full. The latter is our concern here.

Why would a lender accept a $130,000 payoff when the mortgage amount due is $150,000? Why not insist on the whole amount? The lender can prevent the sale by such insistence and hold your nose to the grindstone, demanding that you pay. Why would a lender, part of a group not well known for their generosity, accept less than it's owed?

The answer is that you've prepared a back door in advance. You prepared by showing that lender that the consequences of not accepting a short payoff would be far more dire than accepting it. How can you do this? It takes advance planning and some courage.

Making Yourself Less Desirable

A friend of mine once had a car loan from one of the independent lenders who make such loans through dealers. He kept up his payments assiduously for a year or two and then wanted to sell. He found a buyer and brought her into the lender and said he wanted her to assume his car loan.

The lender carefully looked over the loan history, saw that my friend had never been late in making a payment, smiled, and said, "No." That was it. The lender said there was no advantage in letting someone else take over the loan, not with the wonderful borrower my friend had proven himself to be.

My friend lost the sale and was furious. So he stopped making payments. The lender let a month slide, but at the end of two was threatening to repossess the car.

My friend told the lender that he'd see the car wrecked before he let it go back to the lender.

Then he found another buyer and brought her in. She liked the car and wanted to assume the loan. She had good credit.

This time the loan officer looked at my friend, who had not recently made any payments and who was threatening to wreck the car and compared him to this new well-qualified person. He shook her hand and welcomed her to the company.

No, I'm not recommending you do this with your car. However, it does illustrate a point. Lenders are businesspeople and they make cold-hearted business decisions. If you make one alternative more profitable to them than another, you'll very likely get their attention and get them to "do the right thing."

I have another friend who got caught up in the great real estate crash in Los Angeles in the early 1990s. She had a beautiful home. But when the defense industries cut back, she lost her job and couldn't make her payments (she and about 200,000 others).

Suddenly, once-expensive homes such as hers were for sale all over and prices were plummeting. By the time she realized she couldn't keep the house, it was worth $20,000 less than her mortgage payoff. She contacted the lender who, true to form, didn't want to even discuss the matter with a borrower who had never missed or been late with a payment.

So she stopped making payments.

Mortgage lenders, particularly in a tough market, are far more lenient than auto lenders. They let her go six months without a payment before threatening foreclosure. But when they did, she called them up and explained the situation. Her house was worth less than she owed. If they foreclosed and took it back, they wouldn't get any more for it than she would. And in the interim if she moved out (walked), vandals might do all types of damage to it that might cost the lender thousands more in fix-up costs. Plus there were the costs of the foreclosure itself.

Then she proposed a compromise. She would auction off the property. It would go quickly on a weekend to the highest bidder. And the lender would accept a short sale and a short payoff.

The lender said it would think about it. But it didn't say no.

So my friend went ahead with the sale, making it contingent upon the lender's acceptance. Sure enough, she found a buyer, as it turned out for $15,000 less than the mortgage amount and presented the terms as a fait accompli to the lender. Without a word the lender accepted the short payoff.

ote

There can be undesirable tax consequences of having the lender accept a short payoff. Check with your tax adviser.

How Far Can I Plan Ahead?

In our example, my friend planned ahead about six months. However, she could have planned ahead all the way from the time she bought the property. The fact is that some lenders are more amenable to accepting short payoffs than others are. And some lenders won't accept them at all.

She might have contacted agents to find out which lenders were more lenient (in terms of short payoffs) in her area and then applied for a mortgage from them.

ote

Lenders change hands (are bought out) and change policies over time. Getting a lenient lender, as described, at the time you purchase does not automatically guarantee the lender will be lenient at the time you are forced to sell.

How Do I Auction Off My Property?

We've seen how to convince a lender to accept a short payoff from an auction. But how do you handle the auction itself?

There's essentially very little to it. You pick a date, typically a Sunday. Then you advertise that on that Sunday morning at your home you will sell the property to the highest bidder. And you do.

No, it's not quite that simple, but almost. You must advertise widely in newspapers, bulletin boards, flyers, and so on so that enough people see your advertisement to perk up local interest. You must contact as many real estate agents as possible to let them know what you plan. (If you have some equity, you can tell them you'll even pay at least a partial commission.) And you may want to include a "reserve," a price below which you will not sell (although this tends to reduce interest in the sale).

Usually, a two-week period between the start of advertising and the auction itself is optimum. And you'll want to get a real estate attorney to help you with the paperwork and to be sure that you sell subject to approval by the lender.

Be aware, however, that there are competitors. Professional real estate auctioneers are everywhere these days and buyers usually prefer to purchase from a professional rather than from an amateur. (Also, many books on the subject are available in the bookstores—you may want to check it out.)

What about a "Deed in Lieu"?

Thus far we've been talking about twisting the lender's arm to accept a short payoff sale. However, there is another, though probably less desirable, alternative—giving the property directly to the lender. It's called giving a deed to the lender in lieu of foreclosure and should be considered only as a last and desperate measure.

A deed in lieu often does go on your credit report and while not nearly so bad as a foreclosure, is still bad enough. It alerts future lenders that you, essentially, were not able to keep the property.

Many lenders will refuse to accept a deed in lieu. They would rather foreclose on you.

Some lenders, however, fearing the period of time when you abandon the property and when they get possession (during which very expensive vandalism may take place) and wishing to save the costs of the foreclosure process, may accept it. A smart lender who sees that the owner has no other way out will accept a deed in lieu. Unfortunately, many lenders will not.

You'll probably have to use extreme pressure on the lender, such as described previously, to get it to accept a deed in lieu. But if the lender does, it's yet another backdoor option. (Again, check with your tax adviser.)

What about a Lease Option?

The final back door that we will consider is the lease option. Again, preparation for this should take place at the time you purchase your home, although if you're lucky, it can fall into place later on.

The lease option is a time-honored method of disposing of real estate other than using an outright sale. It combines renting with selling. It can be used when you need to get out of a property you've purchased by the back door. Here's how it works:

In a standard sale, the seller gives the buyer title and possession of the property in exchange for cash and notes. You, the seller are out and a new buyer is in. It's clean and clear-cut.

In a lease option, the seller rents the property to the potential buyer with the written understanding that after a specified period of time, typically two to three years, the "tenant" will purchase the home. Usually, part of the rent goes toward the down payment, making the ultimate purchase easier. You, the seller, continue to hold title. But you've got someone in the property paying rent so that you can make your mortgage payments. And, hopefully, with a little luck in a few years this person will qualify for a new mortgage, pay you the balance of your equity, and buy the property.

In essence, the lease option is like a delayed sale—a back door that opens very slowly.

How Can I Prepare for a Lease Option?

As we noted in Chapter 2, when an investor buys a property, she looks at it both in terms of future resale potential as well as the ability to successfully rent it out until resale time. Thus far we have focused almost exclusively on the resale aspect. Now let's consider rentability.

The fact is that high home sales do not necessarily mean high rents and slow home sales do not necessarily mean low rents. Indeed, the rental market often works inversely with regard to the sales market. When homes are selling quickly, it's hard to find tenants (because many of them have become buyers), and similarly when homes are selling poorly, tenants are plentiful (because rather than buy, many people are holding back and renting).

Thus, in general, at the very time you want to give a lease option (in a bad home resale market), it's likely that things will work for you and there will be a plentiful tenant market. No, it doesn't always work that way, but it often does.

This doesn't mean, however, that you can always rent your house for enough money to cover your mortgage, insurance, taxes, and maintenance costs. Indeed, in most cases you'd be lucky to cover a fraction of that total amount. In today's market, rental prices have not kept pace with sales prices. The truth is that while, for example, your monthly payments may come close to $2,000 a month, your potential rental income could be as low as half that. Then the question becomes, can you afford to do a lease option while taking money out of your pocket each month to make up the deficit in monthly payments? (Actually, the rent on a lease option is usually a little higher than the going market rate, for some of it is applied to a future down payment.)

One way to protect yourself is to plan ahead at the time you buy and do as investors do: check out the rental market.

How Do I Check Out the Rental Market?

I can guarantee you that one thing that homebuyers almost never do is check out the rental market in the area in which they are making their purchase. Yes, they'll look into comparable sales to help establish price. But they'll not determine what the house could potentially rent for. Renting, after all, is the furthest thing from their minds—unless they are considering a back door.

Checking out the rental market before you buy doesn't take long and is a worthwhile thing to do. You'll quickly learn that rental prices are influenced by a variety of factors that often are different from those that influence sales prices. These include:

- Demand for rental housing

- Condition and age of nearby competitive rentals

- Quality of likely tenants

To check out the rental market potential for a home you are considering, you need to pay attention to all three of the following critical points. Let's consider each separately.

What's the Local Demand for Rental Housing?

Some areas just don't have many tenants. For example, small towns and some neighborhoods off the beaten track don't attract many renters. If there are no industries or large companies nearby providing jobs, there may likewise be relatively few tenants available. Few tenants normally mean lower rents.

On the other hand, some areas have large tenant populations. If there's a college campus nearby, you can be assured of a steady stream of tenants, although not necessarily ones with the ability to pay high rents. Having manufacturing or commercial industry nearby is also likely to produce tenants, this time often with the ability to pay higher rents. Even having a commercial center or shopping mall not far off can produce a larger tenant pool.

What's the Competition Like?

The rental competition is by type of housing. If you have a single-family house (SFH), you are in competition with all other SFHs plus a few of the bigger condos/town houses. If you are considering purchasing a condo/town house, from a rental perspective you'll be in competition with all similar dwellings plus a few of the smaller houses.

Typically, the competition is based on rental rates. Apartments rent for less than condos. Condos rent for less than town houses. Town houses rent for less than SFHs. And SFHs rent for the most money.

Some areas have lots of rental housing. Other areas have very little. If you're buying an SFH, you've got the best market in terms of price.

However, if there are lot of town houses and condos around, would-be tenants for your home might just be willing to accept less living space to pay less.

Similarly, if you're considering purchasing a condo or a town house and there are a lot of apartments nearby, would-be tenants may again accept less to pay less.

Thus, what you should do is to take a morning and find out what the true rental competition is like. Your first stop should be a real estate agent who specializes in rentals. (Most agents don't want to bother with rentals, preferring sales instead. But a few do specialize in rentals, realizing that along the way they may convert a tenant into a buyer or a landlord into a seller.)

Go to a rental specialist agent and describe the house you are considering purchasing. You don't need to beat around the bush, just describe the exact house. Then ask, "If I hire you to rent this house for me, what rental rate can I expect to get?"

You've now placed the issue squarely where this expert should be able to handle it. If the agent is indeed knowledge-able, he or she ought to be able to pinpoint the rent to within $25 a month. Typically, the agent will say something like, "You can rent it tomorrow for $900 a month. If you want to try to get $950, you would have to wait, perhaps months."

*N*ote

I probably wouldn't pose this question to the agent who is representing me in the purchase. After all, I'm just asking for an opinion and it's too easy to pull a figure out of thin air. Besides, an agent who doesn't specialize in rentals might not know. And it's too easy to influence your purchase decision by claiming an inflated rental rate.

To confirm what the agent told you, you may also want to check out rentals in the local newspaper, particularly the Sunday edition. They are usually listed by area and price. You'll quickly find out what other houses or similar condos are renting for. To be doubly sure, go out to see one or two that seem similar to the property you are considering. You'll have your confirmation.

What's the Quality of Tenants?

We've already touched on this. Are the likely tenants going to be college students or professional workers? College students tend to be harder on a rental than professionals.

Are the tenants likely to be big families (almost certainly the case if you're attempting to rent a house with four or more bedrooms) or couples or individuals? Children are really rough on a house.

Ask the agent how much trouble he or she has been having with tenants who don't pay. Some areas, particularly if there's an economic recession going on, have higher rates of bad tenants. (The worst tenant, of course, is the one who won't pay and won't get out!)

Keep in mind that your ability to discriminate between tenants has been greatly reduced by antidiscrimination laws. In general, you can refuse to rent to a tenant who doesn't meet your income and credit standards, applied fairly to all. But you cannot refuse to rent because a tenant has children or is of a particular gender, race, religion, or age, or has a medical problem or handicap. You could be liable for big bucks in damages if you do.

What you want are high-quality tenants, those who pay the rent on time and keep the property in great shape. If it turns out, however, that in your area there are mostly low-quality tenants, those who pay late and leave a mess, you'll have to factor in extra money to account for evictions and cleanup afterward, sometimes a very costly proposition.

Comparing Rental Income with Expenses

Once you've considered all the tenant factors, now create a potential income/expense statement for renting with an investor's eye. Here are your likely costs on a lease option:

- Mortgage payments

- Insurance

- Taxes

- Repairs

- Maintenance

- Management fee to agent for handling rental

---

*N*ote

You can substantially reduce the cost of the last three items by doing repairs, maintenance, and renting yourself. But don't think there won't be some cost if nothing more than faucet washers and newspaper advertising. Usually, there's lots more.

Now look at your likely rental income and compare the two.

With a lease option you're looking at two to three years (at least) of renting out the property until a sale can take place. If it's going to cost you $1,000 a month out of pocket to do this, it's probably no back door at all. On the other hand, if it costs you only a few hundred dollars or it's a breakeven, it may be a very good back door indeed.

Remember: With a lease option you can charge a bit higher rent than market rates. A tenant will pay mainly because you're allowing a portion of the rent to eventually be applied to the down payment.

If you're looking to purchase a house in an area with a favorable rental market, you've just found your back door—the lease option. On the other hand, if the area's rental market is very unfavorable, then perhaps you should consider a different back door . . . or a different area.

What's the Bottom Line?

Ultimately, very few people take the time to build a back door into the purchase a home. It's not exactly fun work. And you may encounter resistance from the agent and the seller as well who may say, "You're buying for today, for the here and now. Who knows what can happen in the future? Five or ten years from now we may be at war, or the land could have fallen into the sea. Why worry about it today?"

You may be made to feel foolish about your concerns; you may even be belittled for them. That, however, doesn't mean they aren't valid or real.

It was one thing to forget about the future when we all believed that real estate home prices were going to go up and up forever. But as we all know, those days of innocence are long gone. We all should realize now that what can go up also can go down. And it's the wise person who prepares in advance for the cold days of winter.

Look for assumable loans. They are generally your best and easiest back door. They are somewhat difficult to locate, particularly these days. But you may find a seller with one and when you do, look toward negotiating a "one-time assumable" second mortgage. You probably never will need this, but if you do, you'll thank heaven for the day you got one.

Also be prepared to wrangle with your lender, if necessary, to get a shorter payoff. This is a desperation move, but it sometimes works. Combined with an auction or other device such as a "deed in lieu," it can also allow you to gracefully back out.

Finally, don't just check out the selling market, check out the rental market as well. Try to buy in an area where the rental market is strong. It could save the day later on when you want to offer a lease option.

Every fire-safe home should have a back door. And every financially safe one should have a financial back door, too.

---

*C*hecklist for Keeping a Back Door Open
_____

❏   Have you anticipated a downturn in the market?

❏   Have you anticipated an unexpected financial difficulty?

❏   What about unanticipated personal problems?

❏   Is the mortgage assumable?

❏   Have you looked hard trying to find one?

❏   Is the second mortgage assumable?

❏   Have you put aside any thoughts of "walking" as a back door?

❏   Have you considered an auction, if necessary?

❏   Can you "push" a lender into a short payoff?

❏   Would you consider a "deed in lieu"?

❏   Would you try a lease/option?

❏   Have you investigated the potential rental market?

Back doors are not always pleasant. The more checks, the more you're willing to face reality when times get tough.

CHAPTER 11

Don't Restrict Your Ability to Resell

When we buy a home, must of us just assume that we will be unfettered when it comes time to resell. Want to sell? Place a "For Sale" sign on your front lawn and off you go, right?

Not necessarily. Depending on how you originally structured the purchase of the home, the resale can be difficult or easy. In the past chapter we discussed creating a back door, a way out, so to speak, that would allow you to exit gracefully from a property if hard times fell. In this chapter we're going to look at restrictions that you may inadvertently place on yourself at the time you buy that keep you from more easily reselling later, even in a good market.

As always, we're concerned with how you structure the deal and financing when you purchase, looking forward to your ability to resell later on. And we're casting out with an investor's eye.

Does Your Mortgage Have a Prepayment Clause?

Back in the 1960s and 1970s, most mortgages had a prepayment clause. This stated that if you paid the mortgage off prematurely (before the 30 years it had to run), you'd pay a penalty, often a severe one, typically six months' worth of interest.

The idea was to discourage sellers from paying off the mortgage early. It enabled mortgage companies to keep what, at the time, were mostly well-paying mortgages on the books. In addition, in those days, most conventional loans (nongovernment insured or guaranteed) were fully assumable. When you wanted to sell, you'd just have the buyer assume the existing loan. Pay a small fee, fill out a few documents, and it was a done deal.

In other words, the lenders wanted to keep that mortgage on the property. Interest rates didn't fluctuate much and weren't a big concern. Rather, rollovers—the cost of taking back the cash from a mortgage and then sending it out on a new one—were the big issues with the lenders. They preferred someone else assuming the existing loan to having it paid off.

When interest rates shot up in the late 1970s and early 1980s, most lenders reconsidered assumptions and prepayment clauses in mortgages. Suddenly, it was not to their advantage to have the next buyer assume the low-interest rate of the existing mortgage. In fact, large inventories of low-interest-rate mortgages forced many lenders out of business in those high-interest days. All of a sudden the lenders wanted to call in those mortgages so they could issue new high-rate ones.

Thus they turned the tables around. They eliminated the assumability of most conventional mortgages (so they would have to be paid off whenever the home was sold) and they also eliminated the prepayment clause, thus *encouraging* sellers to refinance and pay off existing low-interest-rate loans.

Since the early 1980s, therefore, we have had conventional loans mostly without prepayment penalties or assumability (as discussed in detail in the past chapter). Indeed, most homebuyers today don't even know what the term *prepayment clause* means.

However, things always seem to change and when they change, they come full circle. Once again, lenders are inserting prepayment clauses in new mortgages. Today, we are in a period of relative stability in mortgage interest rates. As of this writing they haven't dropped much below 7 percent or risen much above 8 percent in more than a decade.

Furthermore, a phenomenon has occurred called the "no-fee mortgage." As part of the competition in the field and to obtain new loans from borrowers, lenders have been adding their fees into the interest rate charged and calling the mortgages "no fee loans." It works like this: The market rate might be 7.5 percent and there might $5,000 in fees to get a new mortgage. So the lender now says, pay me 8 percent and I won't charge you the $5,000 fee. It sounds like there's no fee and if you already have a loan higher than 8 percent, you might say, "Why not?"

This has led to a phenomenon where today some borrowers jump from mortgage to mortgage, sometimes as many as four or five times a year, always working to get an ever-lower interest rate. Because there are no fees, there's no reason not to switch. And because there are no fees, some people will change mortgages just to get a reduction of one- or two-tenths of a percent in the interest rate! Needless to say this has lenders pulling their hair out. No sooner do they get a mortgage on the books than the borrower goes to a different lender, gets a different mortgage, and pays the last one off. It's like playing musical chairs in the mortgage lending business and a lousy way to run a mortgage company.

In response, the lenders have come up with an old-fashioned solution—bring back the prepayment penalty. If a borrower has to pay a penalty to pay back a loan, suddenly it's far more difficult to switch.

Because it has been given up for only two decades, it's not nearly so easy to reestablish. Most buyers don't know what it is and when they learn about it (and learn that competing lenders may not require it), they refuse to accept it.

Thus, many of today's lenders have upped the ante. They are now paying borrowers to accept prepayment penalties! That's right, some lenders will offer borrowers cash payments of $500 to $2,500 to accept a prepayment penalty of from three to ten years. You accept the agreement, you get the cash. But if you need to sell and pay off the loan within the restricted period, you pay a hefty penalty, often more than six months' worth of interest. In addition, unlike the mortgages back in the early days that offered assumability with prepayment, today's mortgages generally offer little to no assumability.

If you think this is a case of lenders wanting it all their way, you wouldn't be far wrong.

Therefore, when you are purchasing a home, you may be asked to accept a prepayment penalty. You may even be offered cash to do so.

Should I Accept Cash for a Prepayment Penalty?

Before you accept, remember that concept of an escape hatch, a back door. Yes, you may not be thinking about selling the property within the next ten years. But what if something totally unforeseen happens next year and you do have to sell? With a prepayment penalty, you're up the creek. Now, not only do you have all the other costs of the sale, but you've got a huge penalty to pay to the lender as well.

Yet, you may say, what about the cash the lender is willing to pay for the prepayment privilege? Doesn't that balance things out?

It could, if the cash payment were big enough. Most of the mortgages I've seen, however, offer piddling little in terms of cash come-on in exchange for huge penalties in the event of prepayment. In other words, yes, you may get a few hundred dollars to allow the lender to insert a prepayment clause. But that clause could cost you many thousands of dollars if you have to sell and pay off the mortgage.

For myself, if the prepayment clause were to cost me, say $5,000 within the next three years, I'd want the mortgage company to come up with at least $2,500 as an inducement. I'd be wagering $2,500 against $5,000 that I wouldn't need to sell (and pay off the mortgage) within that time frame. I'd like those odds.

Most that I've seen, however, offer $500 cash against a $5,000 prepayment penalty if I sell within the next five to seven years. Those odds simply are not good enough for me. Are they for you?

The bottom line is that the prepayment clause restricts your ability to resell. No, it does not prevent you from reselling, but it does discourage you and it does take away a substantial amount of your profit if you do. The general rule here is quite simple, avoid mortgages with prepayment clauses.

Does Your Mortgage Have a Balloon Payment?

Most of us, when we buy a home, are concerned with reducing that monthly payment to as small a figure as possible. Along the way several alternatives may be suggested to us by our agent, the seller, or others involved in the deal. One of these may be a mortgage with a balloon payment.

"Balloon payment" is an innocuous term hinting of gaily colored balloons at an amusement park. Nothing could be further from the truth. A balloon payment means that one payment is bigger than all the others—sometimes huge.

On the other hand, a balloon payment can reduce your mortgage payments in the following manner. Let's say you have a $20,000 second mortgage for five years at 9 percent interest. To fully amortize that mortgage (fully pay it off in equal monthly installments), you'd need to pay about $415 a month. That's in addition to your first mortgage, insurance, taxes, homeowner's fees, and whatever else you may need to pay monthly. It can be a significant burden.

But what if an agent says to you, "I can reduce that amount. Instead of paying it off fully, why not just pay the interest. The interest-only portion is $150 a month. I can save you roughly $265 a month in payments."

Wouldn't you grab it? That would cut your payments on the second mortgage by more than half. And that's for every month for the next five years.

Of course, whenever things seem too good to be true, they generally are. The trouble is that at the end of the five-year period, you won't have paid back a dime on the original mortgage principal. Remember, you'd be paying only interest. Therefore, you'd still owe $20,000. And you'd owe the full amount anytime you sold the property prior to five years. That's the balloon payment.

But it can get even more interesting. Now what if the seller says, "I'm desperate to sell. I'll tell you what, I'll make that a second mortgage with no payments at all. Your monthly payments will be zero!"

Now that's a hard loan to beat. But when you ask about the interest, the seller says, "Don't worry about that. We'll just tack it onto the principal. You can pay it all off five years from now."

Doesn't sound quite so good. That's because it's not. You'd be adding 9 percent interest per year compounded to the mortgage. You'd owe more than half as much as you originally borrowed (more than $30,000) by year five! That's the balloon.

Should I Gamble on a Big Balloon?

Do mortgages like these actually occur? You better believe they do. In fact, investors sometimes specifically go looking for them, gambling that they'll be able to resell for enough money to handle the payoff by the time it's due (or beforehand).

But do you want to take that gamble? Do you want to risk not only not having a back door, but putting bars on the front door, making it ever more difficult to get out in case you have to?

No doubt there's a place for a balloon payment mortgage. I've taken many myself. But they are a gamble. If I have to sell early or if I can't resell or refinance when they come due, I could be in big trouble. I might even lose the property as the holder of that second mortgage could foreclose. (In most cases, though certainly not all, you can negotiate with the holder of the second mortgage to roll it over for a few more years, usually by using the incentive of a higher interest rate.)

Used properly, a balloon mortgage has its place in real estate transactions. However, it can cause all types of problems if you're not prepared to deal with that balloon when it comes due or if your plans change and you have to unexpectedly sell early.

Do You Have a Short-Term Mortgage?

This is a variation of the balloon mortgage, however, played for higher stakes with first mortgages. (The order of the mortgage determines who gets paid off when there is a foreclosure sale—the holder of the first mortgage gets all money due first. Then any money that is left over goes to the holder of the second mortgage. Any money remaining then goes to the holder of the third mortgage and so on. Only when all the mortgages are fully paid does the borrower get what's left. Thus, first mortgages are considered the most secure.)

Short-term mortgages have been in vogue for about a decade. In fact, in some areas they represent more than a third of all mortgages issued.

They work like this: For instance, you're getting a mortgage for $100,000. You naturally want the lowest interest rate. The lender says it will give you 8 percent at 30 years. But if you accept a ten-year payoff, it will drop the rate to 7¾ percent. And if you accept a three-year payoff, it will drop the interest rate to 7¼ percent.

You get the idea—the shorter the mortgage term, the lower the interest rate. Of course, in all cases the payments are made as if the mortgage were for the full 30 years. You pay interest and principal as if you'd gotten a fully amortized loan. It's just that at a designated date in the future, there's a balloon with the entire remaining balance due.

Talk about not having a back door! This is like having a precipice yawning out behind you. I've seen people get a five-year due date and go blithely along until "suddenly" at year five they realize they owe the entire first mortgage amount, often hundreds of thousands of dollars. (It happens like this: your payments might be continuing along at $1,000 a month in November, $1,000 in December, and then $150,000 in January when the mortgage comes due!) Suddenly, it's a scramble to refinance, or if that's not possible, to sell quickly and at any cost to avoid foreclosure. Selling under such pressure is obviously not the way to go.

Why Should I Be Forced to Sell?

Of course, you may be asking, why do you have to sell? Why not refinance at the time the mortgage comes due? Why can't refinancing be my back door?

Sometimes your financial situation will have changed to the point where you no longer can qualify for a new mortgage. Plus, even if you can qualify, there are usually significant fees to pay. (Remember, if you opted for a "no-fee" mortgage, you're paying a higher interest rate.)

Trading off the length of a mortgage for a lower interest rate can force you to resell early and accept a lower price to get a quick sale. It's just a different kind of restriction.

By the way, sometimes you can get a "rollover" provision put into an early-payoff mortgage. The rollover says that at the time of the payoff, if you don't (or can't) pay it off, the mortgage automatically converts to (usually an ugly) adjustable rate mortgage. That means you end up paying a higher-than-market interest rate. But at least you don't have to worry about losing the property to foreclosure. For the privilege of getting this ugly adjustable, you usually pay additional points or fractions of interest rate when you first get the early payoff mortgage.

Are You in a Restrictive Homeowners Association?

Today a large percentage of homes are part of a planned community including a homeowners association. All condos and co-ops have these and many single-family residences also belong to them.

Homeowners associations, also called HOAs, are responsible for common areas such as walkways, recreational facilities, sometimes front yards, and so on. They are also responsible for maintaining whatever standards were originally put into place as part of the creation of the housing development—the Conditions, Covenants, and Restrictions (CC&Rs). And this can lead to problems later on.

Sometimes HOAs can restrict your ability to resell years down the road. Decades ago, some communities had restrictions against reselling to people of different races and religions. These have all been ruled unconstitutional and even if they are still part of the CC&Rs, they are unenforceable.

Restrictions may apply, however, to the age of the person to whom you can resell or whether or not they have children. Generally speaking, if the age of 80 percent or more of the membership of the HOA is, for example, 55, it can call itself a retirement community and restrict sales to older people, those without children.

While this may enhance your ability to resell later on to a retiree, it eliminates your ability to sell to younger people. In effect, it cuts out more than half of all potential buyers.

In some co-ops, the board (which is equivalent to the HOA) may restrict your ability to sell to someone who doesn't have a certain minimum income level.

In many condominium associations, the HOA will refuse to allow you to place a "For Sale" sign on the lawn in front of your unit. This means it's more difficult for potential buyers to learn that your property is for sale and to find it once they do. (Usually, but not always, you can put a sign in your front window.) Again this restricts your ability to resell easily.

When you're considering the purchase of a home and you learn that it has an HOA, it would be well worth your while to investigate to determine what, if any, restrictions will apply when it comes time for you to resell. If the restrictions are too severe, you may want to look elsewhere.

Look before You Leap

There are all types of ways that your ability to resell can be restricted. We've only looked at a few here. But the common denominator running through all of them is that to avoid these restrictions, you must act before you buy. Either have the restrictions removed or modified . . . or purchase elsewhere. (Also check Chapter 14.)

---

*C*hecklist for Unrestricted Resale

❑ Have you checked your mortgage for a prepayment clause?

❑ If your mortgage does have a prepayment clause, will your lender offer you a bonus?

❑ Is the bonus really worthwhile?

❑ Does your mortgage have a balloon payment?

❑ Is it many years off?

❑ Will it automatically refinance in the worst case?

❑ Is your HOA restrictive?

❑ Is it realistic to consider changing the HOA's rules?

You want the least restrictive checks. The more you tie yourself in to a mortgage/home, the more difficult to extricate yourself down the road.

CHAPTER 12

Evaluating Property for Future Profit

In many ways the theme of this book is that you make your profit when you *buy*, not when you sell. If you buy right, then you almost can't lose when it comes time to sell. In this chapter we're going to work backward. We're going to look at what it will cost us to sell to get a better idea of what we can afford to pay when we buy.

What If You Have to Resell Tomorrow?

Here's a useful exercise that I suggest for everyone who is considering a home purchase. Imagine for a moment that you must put up your home for sale tomorrow. What will you get for it? How much will your cost of selling be? Most important, will you lose, break even, or make money on the deal?

Before we delve into this in detail, let's remember that we're not talking about something such as buying a car. Everyone knows that when you buy a car, particularly a new car, the minute you drive it off the lot it's worth about 25 percent less than it was the minute before. We all know it, expect it, and accept it.

Here, however, we're not talking about a consumer item. Here we're talking about an investment. (If you're not sure of the difference, reread Chapters 1 and 2.) Here, we should expect, at the least, to break even and, hopefully, to do better than that and make a profit.

But will we?

If we have to sell tomorrow, can we net out enough from our house to break even? To show a profit? If not, why not?

In this chapter we're going to look at what it will cost to resell that house that we are considering buying and once we've arrived at an appropriate figure, determine the *maximum* we should pay today to ensure that we'll do well at resale time.

Buying the Typical House

To have a consistent example, we're going to purchase, for the sake of this chapter, a typical house. The median price of a home in the United States these days is around $120,000. So we'll assume our seller is asking $125,000 for the house. (Sellers almost universally ask more than their house is worth because they know buyers will make lower offers.) We'll assume we can buy it for $120,000.

Now the question is, "If we had to turn around and resell this property the day after tomorrow, presumably for what it's worth, $120,000, how much money would we lose on the deal?" Another way to put it is, "How much less than $120,000 would we need to pay for this house today to at least break even reselling it tomorrow?" You may find the answer to this question fascinating, and it could turn around your whole way of thinking about what you want to pay for a home.

What Does It Cost to Sell with an Agent?

The biggest selling expense, of course, is the agent's commission, and we'll get to that shortly. But first, remember that other costs are always involved in the selling of a property. These are

going to be part of the resale whether you use an agent or sell
by yourself and they include the following.

Escrow Fees

In most parts of the country these days, the sale of real estate
involves an escrow, which is an independent third party, usually a company, which acts as a holder and conduit. The escrow
holds all documents and monies until they need to be distrib-
uted. It also receives and transmits documents as necessary to
complete the transaction. Escrow fees are normally based on
the selling price of the property.

We'll assume $500.

Title Insurance Fees

This guarantees that you're giving the buyer clear title.
Depending on the locale, sometimes you pay the entire amount,
sometimes the buyer pays it, and sometimes it's split. However
it comes down, you won't pay twice because once you were a
buyer of the property and now you're a seller. Like escrow fees,
these are based on the property's value.

Again we'll assume $500.

Attorneys' Fees

Attorneys are commonly used on the East Coast to facilitate
a sale, used far less often on the West Coast and midcountry
states.

We'll assume $400.

Prorations

These aren't fees, but instead are your portion of the taxes,
insurance, assessments, or other costs that are paid monthly,
semiannually, or annually. You are charged for that portion of
these costs that accrued to you while you owned the property

right up until the date of sale. Their amount can vary enormously depending on the time of year. Taxes, for example, are usually paid twice annually; if the next payment is due shortly, your tax proration will be quite high.

Because you only pay for the time you actually use the property, we won't assume any cost here.

Document Fees

These are usually minor, typically under $100. They are used to pay notary fees and mailing costs of documents necessary to complete the transaction.

We'll assume $50.

Inspection Fees

Typically, you will need to provide a termite clearance and pay for a home inspection. The termite clearance should be minimal, for you presumably had one just a short while earlier when you bought the property. The home inspection should be $250 to $300. Of course, if there should be some work required to get the clearance, that could be extra. But, because you've just had the seller do that, it's unlikely, isn't it?

We'll assume $250.

Miscellaneous Costs

There are always going to be other charges from the price of sending a letter by messenger, to having someone come out and fix a broken sprinkler head.

We'll assume $250.

Agent's Commission

The agent's commission is the largest cost. It's important to understand that no matter what an agent may tell you, there's no "set" commission rate. It's all negotiable. The rate can be 1 percent or 10 percent. It's between you and the agent.

It's also important to remember that many agents have a minimum rate. They simply won't take a listing below that rate, because they feel they can't afford to service it properly. Recently, I've seen agents whose minimums vary between 3 percent and 7 percent for residential property.

Given that wide spread, it's only natural to assume that you should enlist the agent who charges the least. Why pay, for example, 7 percent when another agent may only charge 3 percent? The answer is service and, possibly, speed of sale.

Discount agents, those who charge in the 3 percent range, often don't provide the services that agents who charge more do. They may not advertise your property, but instead require that you pay for ads. They may not even show it, leaving that up to you. They may simply place a sign on the property and list with the local multiple listing service. All of which may mean it will take far longer, if ever, to get a sale.

There is, however, another reason to consider paying a full commission and that's speed of sale.

The big advantage that listing has for you is that you tap into the network of agents. Assuming that your broker cobrokes (works with other agents) your property (and you shouldn't have it any other way), all the agents in your area can now bring buyers by and collect a portion of the commission if they make a sale. Because at any given time, probably 90 percent to 95 percent of all buyers are working with agents, when you list with a broker who cobrokes, you're tapping into nearly all of the buyers in your area. You are dramatically increasing your chances for a sale. You should be able to sell quicker. And time, as we all know, is money.

Agents, however, are only human. Although they should bring buyers to homes that are most suited to those buyers, if one well-suited home is listed at 3 percent and a very similar one is listed at 6 percent or 7 percent, which property would you show first? Which might you fail to show at all?

In other words, although technically (and ethically) it shouldn't make any difference, the commission rate may, in reality, be an important factor in getting action on your property. Therefore, I would think twice before opting to pay a lower commission rate. It may be a case of being penny-wise and pound-foolish.

---

*N*ote

A lot of technical issues are involved with getting an agent. To see what they are and what they might end up costing you, check Appendix A.

We'll assume a 6 percent agent commission, or $7,200.

Can You Resell by Yourself?

Obviously, the commission is a healthy chunk of money. It's only natural to wonder if that can't be cut back. For example, what if you don't use an agent and sell on your own? You'll save a bundle, but is that really feasible?

There are really only two reasons that you might want to resell your home by yourself: the first, obviously, is to save money on the real estate agent's commission. The second is to get a quicker sale. Unfortunately, saving the commission, all of it by selling the property yourself, is unrealistic. On the other hand, getting a quicker sale is a real possibility.

Let's be clear—what we're talking about here is reselling on your own, instead of listing with an agent. You find a buyer and conclude the sale of the property.

Sound easy? It's possible to do, but usually it's not so easy as it sounds. The reason has partly to do with some of the services that an agent normally performs and partly with the expectations of buyers.

Real estate agents, in addition to finding buyers for sellers, perform the additional valuable service of being a buffer between the two parties. You can confide the fact that you really don't like the buyer's guts to the agent, and that information will never get out to poison the deal. Similarly, the buyers can confide that they can't stand you, the seller, and you'll never learn of their animosity. The agent keeps things civil and on track.

On the other hand, when you're dealing directly with the buyer, there's no buffer. Your emotions tend to leak out and so do the buyers'. Thus, there's bound to be friction . . . and that makes putting the deal together more difficult. All it really takes is one unguarded word or even a misunderstanding to throw things into a panic.

Because of this, buyers usually don't want to deal directly with sellers. When typical buyers go looking at property, they expect to be serviced by an agent. They expect to be shown different properties and when they find one they like, they expect to have their whims catered to. They expect to be able to confide their concerns about the seller to this middle person who helps keep things on track. When you sell by owner, you don't live up to the buyer's expectations of how a deal should be handled.

Thus, it's definitely harder to sell by owner. It's harder to get buyers to commit and to move forward on a purchase. It's harder to keep the deal going.

You can, however, overcome these problems simply by offering the buyer a better deal. Indeed, buyers well understand that you're selling by yourself to save the not-inconsiderable money on a commission.

To overcome the problems inherent in selling by owner, therefore, most buyers expect that you will cut them in on some of those savings. If you're saving $7,200, a buyer who's willing to purchase directly from you probably expects to get at least $3,600 of that amount, if not all of it!

In other words, the moment you sell by owner, you raise the expectations of getting a bargain in the eyes of potential buyers. After all, why should they bother with the inconvenience and hassle of dealing with you directly if they'll have to pay the same amount for the property as if they're working through an agent? For the same price, the vast majority of buyers would rather deal with an intermediary, an agent. You have to give the buyers a good reason for dealing directly with you.

To reiterate, you can save money on a commission when you sell by owner. But it's unrealistic to think that you can save the entire commission. If there are two similar houses realistically priced at the market rate and one is offered by the owner and the other through an agent, nine times out of ten, buyers will prefer to work with the agent. Consider this a fact. You'll have to give up some of the money you'll save to make the deal—not necessarily all of it, but perhaps as much as half.

Can You Get a Quicker Sale?

On the other hand, if you need to sell immediately, what you want is a quick sale. Selling by owner allows you to offer buyers an opportunity that's likely to lure them in. You can offer them a bargain.

Compare two similar houses offered at market price. One is listed with an agent, yours is not. Now you can cut your price, because you're not selling through an agent. For example, your house is worth $120,000 on the market. (It doesn't matter whether it's listed or not, the market price is the same.) If you were to cut your price by the entire amount you'd be saving on a commission at 6 percent, you could cut it by $7,200. While your neighbor is offering $120,000, you could ask $112,800 and come out the same.

If one thing is a truism in real estate today, it's that buyers are extremely price-conscious. If you can offer a $120,000 house at around $7,000 below the market cost, you can be assured that you will have a lot of interested buyers. If you can offer the same house at even $3,000 or $4,000 below the market rate (because you're saving on the commission), you'll still have a lot of interested buyers.

Therefore, by cutting your price by an amount equal to a portion of what you're saving on the commission, you can expect a quicker sale. Indeed, savvy For Sale By Owner (FSBO) sellers often get the fastest sales in the neighborhood.

Are You Really Able to Sell "FSBO"?

Selling by owner means that you potentially save yourself time and money. But, selling FSBO is not for everyone. It can be a trying chore. Quite frankly, most sellers opt to let an agent do the work, regardless of any benefits they might get by selling themselves. To find out what's involved, check into my book, *The For Sale By Owner Kit,* Dearborn Financial Publishing, Inc., 1995. Also check Appendix B.

We'll assume that you can save part of the commission by doing some of the sales work yourself. We'll reduce the amount paid on commission to half–$3,600.

What's the Total Cost to Resell Tomorrow?

Here are the figures for reselling our $120,000 property:

---

*C*ost to Resell Immediately

Escrow fees	$ 500
Title insurance	500
Attorney's fee	400
Prorations	–0–
Document fees	50
Inspection fee	250
Miscellaneous costs	250
Agent's commission	3,600
	$5,550

Thus, assuming that everything goes pretty much according to plan, it will cost about $5,550 to resell immediately.

How Much Should We Really Pay When We Buy?

If we were an investor who bought with an eye strictly toward profit, therefore, we would not pay $120,000 for this house. We should pay $5,550 less, or $114,450. This would allow us to resell immediately without taking a loss. Any amount lower than $114,450 would allow us to make a profit.

All of which is to say that if we're a wise buyer, we will endeavor to pay at least 5 percent less-than-market price at the time we buy. (Assuming, of course, that we will participate in the resale, thus saving part of the commission. If we plan to pay a full commission, then we should pay roughly 8 percent less-than-market price.)

Buying for less-than-market price helps to ensure that should things turn sour, we will be able to get out quickly. Of course, the market could fall, the house could deteriorate—a hundred things could happen. All of which is to say, we're talking guarantee here. Rather, we're talking a sensible price that any smart investor would pay for a home.

But can we get the seller to take less-than-market price for the house? That's the subject of the next chapter.

*C*hecklist for Evaluation Future Resale

❏   Have you determined your resale costs for an agent?

❏   Have you determined your resale costs for escrow/title?

❏   Have you determined your resale costs for an attorney?

❏   Have you determined your resale costs for prorations?

❏   Have you determined your resale costs for inspections?

❏   Have you added in a figure for miscellaneous costs?

❏   Have you considered reselling by yourself?

❏   Have you SERIOUSLY considered what's involved?

❏   Have you calculated the total cost to sell tomorrow?

❏   Have you subtracted that cost from what you plan to pay?

CHAPTER 13

Getting the Seller to Take Your Price

Buying right usually means buying low. If you pay a high price going in, your chances of selling quickly and for a profit later on are greatly reduced, if not eliminated. As noted in the last chapter, you often need to pay far less than the seller is asking to protect yourself in the event that an emergency occurs and you must resell quickly.

But how do you get the seller to accept what amounts to a lowball offer? Sellers are notorious for insisting on their price. Is it possible to actually get them to take substantially less?

In this chapter we're going to have a quick course on dealing with the seller. We'll take a look at arguments you can use to get a price reduction. And we'll consider terms that might be even better than a lower price.

Is There Only One Right Price to Pay?

At the onset it's important to understand that unlike bottles of catsup, there is no standard house. While every bottle of catsup from a manufacturer may look exactly the same as every other and they may all be priced identically, houses are not clones of one another. Even the same model in the same tract is going to have some differences even if it's nothing more than different color and different landscaping.

Usually, the differences are far more significant. One owner may have upgraded everything in the property. Another may have added an extra room. Yet another may have let the property deteriorate to the point where it looks terrible. And the condition of the property is going to influence its price.

Thus, there is a price *range* for any given home. If the property has been upgraded, is better located, and is in excellent condition, it should bring the top of the range. If it's been let go and has a less desirable location with no upgrades, it should be at the bottom.

So, if you're looking at homes with a market value of $120,000, the range of properties may actually be anywhere from $110,000 to $130,000. It's not unreasonable, therefore, to expect to buy a property in the lower level of the range. And if you fix it up, often doing nothing more than cosmetic improvement, you may be able to sell it in the upper level of the range. Furthermore, sometimes you can convince a seller to sell an upper-range property for a lower-range price, if your arguments are convincing.

How Do I Evaluate the Property?

Evaluating the property to come up with just the right offer is part science and part art. You need to use a sharp pencil, but you also need to use common sense. Here are five areas you must consider:

1. Condition

2. Asking price

3. Owner's motivation

4. Market

5. Competition

We'll consider each separately.

How Do I Evaluate Conditions?

When you're buying, the worse a property looks, usually the better for you. The important issue is to discriminate between cosmetic and serious problems. Cosmetic problems are easy to fix. They involve landscaping, painting, broken glass, patching holes in doors, occasionally replacing a broken appliance or a fixture (such as a cracked toilet bowl or a big chip in a sink), and so on. What's important to understand about cosmetic problems is that they are easy to fix. You can do it yourself typically with a few cans of paint and some elbow grease. A new toilet bowl can be purchased for less than $50. Holes in walls and doors can be patched. Windows can be replaced. A lawn can be seeded, new flowers and shrubs planted. In other words, for a grand or two, you can take a house that is a cosmetic nightmare and turn it into a wonderful dream. And you can do all of this while you're living in it.

On the other hand, more serious problems may include such things as cracked slabs and/or foundations, leaky roofs, broken heaters/air conditioners, leaky water pipes, bad drainage, and so on. These can cost many thousands of dollars to fix and very frequently you can spend the money and the property will not look much different afterward.

What you are looking for is a cosmetically distressed property. Appearance is everything and if a property looks bad, it knocks the price down considerably. In the range we are speaking, a house that shows poorly can be worth 5 percent to 10 percent less than one that shows well. By being a wise buyer and taking advantage of a distressed-looking property, you can often buy low enough to be able to resell quickly (after doing some cosmetic work) for breakeven or, perhaps, even a profit.

But are there cosmetically challenged homes out there?

Of course there are. Many sellers simply don't want to spend a penny to fix up their property when it comes time to sell. And they still want top dollar. Your job is to convince the seller that the condition of the property warrants a lower price. (But don't be too convincing, for the seller may realize that spending a grand or two will increase the sales price significantly and instead of selling to you, may then pop for the fix-up money and try to resell to someone else for a higher price!)

You may also want to read my book, *Find It, Buy It, Fix It!* from Dearborn Financial Publishing, Inc., 1996.

What Can I Deduce from the Asking Price?

A good rule of thumb to remember is that sellers are almost always hung up on price. They generally want the highest price that any similar home in the area has ever sold for. For example, when sellers put a property up for sale, an agent will usually give them a printout of the prices that comparable homes have sold for. Almost without exception, the sellers will go to the highest price and say that's what they want for their property.

Furthermore, sellers are well aware that the price they put on their property is only what they are *asking*. They know that buyers are going to offer less. Therefore, you can usually assume that the seller anticipates selling for something less than the listed price of the property.

When looking for a home to purchase, it is usually a good idea to avoid those homes that are priced in the upper ranges of the market. For example, if you've determined that the average price for a given model in an area is around $120,000, you'd probably be better off avoiding those homes for which the seller is asking above $120,000. If the seller is asking $130,000, for instance, it may mean that the property is in super condition. Even if you were to get the seller to drop $10,000 in price, it would still mean you're paying the average price for the home. Besides, such sellers usually feel they've got a terrific property and don't want to come down in price.

Better to look for homes in the middle to bottom of the range. These tend to be the ones that are more likely to need cosmetic correction. Also, these sellers may have a better sense of what the market will bear.

Two areas to pay special attention to are the length of time the property has been offered for sale and any price reductions. Usually when sellers first list, they are filled with optimism and hope. If you make a lowball offer during the first couple of weeks of a listing, they are less inclined to accept simply because enough time hasn't elapsed for them to begin to feel desperate. They may figure that yours is just the first of many offers. They can afford to wait and see what else comes in. On the other hand, if it's been five months with no offers, I guarantee your lowball offer is going to get serious consideration.

Are You Dealing with a Buyer's Agent?

Most agents, when they represent the seller, feel that it is unethical to let you know how long a property has been listed. (They won't let you look at the listing book to see how long the property has been on the market.) This is an excellent reason you should use a "buyer's agent." This is an agent who works for you, instead of for the seller. A buyer's agent may feel that it is an ethical duty to find out and tell you how long a property has been offered for sale.

Buyers' agents are cropping up more and more across the country, although some areas still have none. It's important to understand that who pays the agent the commission does not determine who that agent works for. Rather, the agent decides if he or she works for seller, buyer, or both. Often the commission due a buyer's agent will be paid for by the seller. (After all, in most cases the seller has listed the property and agreed to pay a commission anyway.)

Besides time, there's also the matter of price reductions. If a house has been offered for five months and is still at the original asking price, it's safe to assume the seller is hanging tough. On the other hand, if the owner has reduced the price each month, it's safe to assume that this owner wants to sell and may be willing to consider a lowball offer.

Look for long listings and price reductions. They often signal the way to a seller who will take a lowball offer.

What Is the Seller's Motivation?

This leads us to the next consideration—the reason the seller wants to sell the property. As any good agent knows, the key to getting a seller to sign an offer is to tap into his or her motivation. In fact, "motivated sellers" are what agents, and you as a buyer, should be looking for. What are the key motivations that will help you? Here's a list.

---

*M*otivated Sellers

- Job transfer—The seller must move quickly to start work in a distant city.

- Job loss—The owners no longer can keep up the payments and are facing foreclosure if they can't sell quickly.

- Divorce—The owners are splitting up and the house must be sold. Frequently, one former spouse wants to "get" the other by selling for less.

- Change of family—The children have grown up and the house is simply too big. This is not a pressing motivation, but is one that encourages sellers to move on. Or there are more children now and the house is too small. This is a compelling motivation.

- Illness—The seller has fallen ill and must leave for health reasons (for example, the seller has developed asthma and must move to a dryer or wetter climate), or because of financial reasons associated with the illness.

- Wants to move up—The sellers have increased their income and now can afford a better neighborhood. This can be used as an argument by pointing out that the current neighborhood is not so good and doesn't warrant the high price the sellers are asking—they may agree!

- Already bought another house—This is a high motivation because the seller probably can't complete the purchase until this home has been sold. In some cases, the seller of this home only has a few weeks to come up with a buyer or may lose the purchase of the next home.

Of course, sellers have other motivations, but these will do. If the sellers are motivated, they will want to sell and usually sell quickly. They will consider any "reasonable" offer and will usually bend over backward to make even an lowball offer seem reasonable. If you can find a motivated seller, you're halfway home in getting your lowball offer accepted.

How Do I Find Out the Seller's Motivation?

That, of course, is the big question. As noted previously, a seller's agent should find it unethical to reveal his or her seller's motivation. Working with a buyer's agent, however, may solve this problem. The buyer's agent may be able to sniff around and come up with the real reason the seller wants out, thus helping you make a lowball offer and get it accepted.

(By the way, if you're looking for a buyer's agent, just ask around. Most agents are seller's agents, but if you're persistent in your questioning, they often can recommend a buyer's agent in your area. Also, buyer's agents often advertise that fact in the yellow pages of the telephone book.)

Another way to find out motivation is to simply ask the seller. Before you make an offer, you'll probably tour the house a couple of times and on at least one of those visits, the chances are excellent you'll meet the seller. Strike up a conversation and after a while, casually ask, "By the way, why are you selling this property?" You can even suggest that you're worried there might be something wrong with it.

Frequently, sellers will blurt out their reasons for selling. It's a job problem or too small a house for the family or whatever. If they're evasive, such as, "We've decided to move on," you might want to suggest reasons, such as, "You mean you've been transferred?"

"No, that's not it."

"You mean you've already bought a house elsewhere?"

"No, my wife has lost her job and we just can't afford the property anymore."

It's amazing what sellers will tell you. Of course, not all are so open-mouthed and some will actually have concocted a cover story that is far from the truth.

If you can't get a straight answer from the agent or the seller, you might ask the neighbors. I always suggest contacting neighbors before buying a home anyway. The reason is the neighbors usually are quite open and can tell you loads about what the area is like. Besides, if you buy, they'll soon be *your* neighbors and you can quickly decide if you can stand to live next to them! Neighbors often are eager to talk about someone who's leaving the neighborhood and also are often surprisingly well informed.

I know some investors who simply won't make an offer on a property unless and until they know exactly why the seller wants to sell it. Often, if all else fails, they will come right out and say something such as, "I'm considering making an offer on your home. But as a matter of principle, I refuse to make offers until I know the real reason the seller wants out. I'm afraid that otherwise, I might end up buying someone else's problem." Usually, the sellers fess up.

How Does the Market Affect My Offer?

The weaker the market, the better the chance that your lowball offer will be accepted. The stronger the market, the less the chance. It's just that simple.

It only stands to reason. In a down market, buyers hold off. During the great real estate recession of the early 1990s, lowball offers were the rule rather than the exception. A seller putting up a house for sale at $120,000 could not expect to get an offer higher than $110,000. Indeed, often the offers at that asking price were below $100,000. And because the market was so bad, the sellers, if motivated, were inclined to accept the lowball. The feeling was that if you didn't accept today's low offer, the next offer tomorrow might be even lower!

On the other hand, times change. As the market perks up, so does sellers' optimism. If sellers read in the newspaper that the market has stabilized, or is turning up, they're going to be reluctant to accept a lowball offer.

If the sellers are regularly getting a lot of people looking at the property and an offer every week or so, they are likewise going to be inclined to hold out. The stronger the market, the weaker your position in getting a lowball offer accepted.

What about the Competition?

In my own purchase of property, I've found homes in which I wanted to live that were just perfect, that were cosmetically distressed, that had a reasonable asking price, and that were offered by highly motivated sellers. And the market, though perhaps not distressed, was certainly not healthy.

Fully confident of my chances of success, I've shown up to present my lowball offer, only to find that I was second in line, or third, or fifth. Sometimes the other offers were for more than mine. Sometimes they were for full price. Sometimes they were even for more than the asking price!

In such circumstances, I usually bow out. The last thing I want to do is to get into a bidding war with other buyers.

It's important to understand that in any market there are lots of buyers, both consumers and investors, out there. And they are doing essentially the same thing as you are. Often they find the same house and come to the same conclusions about it. So just as you're ready to make an offer, so are they.

When this happens, just take it as a compliment. It means you're doing your job. You've found the right house. It's just that others have found it, too. And if they're offering more than you are, substantially more, it only means that they don't have as sharp a pencil as you do. They've got the right house, but the wrong price.

Back off. The last thing you want to do is to pay more than you should. And that will almost certainly happen if you get into a bidding war.

Plenty of other houses are out there. Many of them are in cosmetically distressed conditions, with the right asking price, with motivated sellers in today's market. Just find one before the rest of the crowd does and make your offer all by itself. You've a much better chance of getting the right price accepted.

Note

Sometimes you just have to wait for the right deal to come along. It's usually a mistake to pick a time and say that now you've *got* to buy. Maybe the right house just isn't available at the right price. Better to wait than to jump into the market prematurely.

Put It All Together

As part of your evaluation process, you must consider the five elements and make them work to your advantage. When you do, you should be able to get the right price.

1. Condition—look for cosmetically distressed properties.

2. Asking price—look for a price in the middle to bottom of the range.

3. Owner's motivation—seek out highly motivated sellers.

4. Market—know what the market is and understand if it will help or hinder you.

5. Competition—be prepared for others doing the same thing as you. Try to find the right property before they do.

How Do I Get the Seller to Accept My Offer?

Thus far we've been evaluating the property to find just the right home on which to make an offer. Once we've done that, what arguments can we use to get the seller to accept our offer?

Negotiating real estate is a fine art and there are those who have been in the business for many years who say they are still learning. There are dozens of "rules" and even more strategies and tactics. Some work, some work some of the time, and some never work. Here we're going to touch on just a few to get you started.

Always Insist on a Time Limit

When you make an offer, you want the seller to seriously consider it. So does your agent. But sometimes your agent may not give you good advice. Sometimes an agent will say, "Let's give the sellers a couple of days to chew on this."

Bad idea. In a couple of days another, better offer may come in. The seller is under no obligation to consider only your offer because it came in first. The seller will consider any and all offers.

Therefore, my feeling is that it's a good idea to set a time limit, typically one day. (All sales agreements provide for your giving the seller a certain amount of time to accept the offer.) The agent should be able to reach the seller within that amount of time and the seller should be able to consider and either accept, reject, or counter your offer.

Get the Seller to Invest Time

Having said that it's important to set a time limit, it's likewise important to get the seller to invest time in your offer. It's a truism that the more time we invest in anything, the more we want to see it through to a successful conclusion. Sellers who spend three days in negotiating with you are far more likely to be interested in getting a deal than sellers who spend three minutes and can simply blow off the deal.

Therefore, always instruct your agent (if he or she presents the offer) to ask for a counter, if and when the seller rejects your original offer. It almost doesn't matter what the counter offer is. The idea is to keep negotiations alive. When Presidents Jimmy Carter and Bill Clinton were negotiating Middle East peace treaties, often the negotiations themselves proved fruitless. But simply keeping the negotiators at the table got the participants to invest in the process. And that eventually led to agreements. (Of course, whether or not the agreements were later honored is a different story.)

You can then reject the seller's counter and counter on your own—perhaps a bit higher, perhaps with different terms. As the negotiations continue, often new information about the seller's goals will come out and you can change your offer to accommodate them. For example, it may turn out that the seller owns the property free and clear and plans to invest the money in a CD. Instead of raising your price, you might offer a first mortgage at slightly higher-than-market rates. This is a very secure position and it will yield far more than the seller could get on a CD. Suddenly, your offer might be received far more warmly.

The idea is to get the seller to invest as much time as possible. The more time, the more likely the chance of success.

Don't Be Fooled by the "Pie" Analogy

After some negotiating, almost inevitably someone will bring up the pie analogy. You know it. It goes something like this. "You [the buyers] are offering only so much money. No matter how we divide it up, there just isn't enough to go around. So there's no deal."

Find a way to make the pie bigger, without your offering more money. Maybe instead of cash, the seller will accept a second mortgage. The pie is the same size, only now you've got additional financing and don't have to come up with so much money.

Take the Easy Problems First

In any negotiations there are going to be big differences and little differences. If you concentrate on the big differences, you are almost certain to lose. The reason is because they are *big* differences. For example, you offer $105,000, the seller wants $125,000. That's a big difference. Concentrate on that and there's no deal.

On the other hand, what about possession. You want a 90-day escrow, the seller wants 30 days, so you compromise at 45 days. Or what about termite repair work. You want the seller to pay for both repair and prevention. The seller agrees to pay only for repair. You go along.

You get the idea. You find areas of compromise and pretty soon you're agreeing everywhere. Suddenly, the deal seems like it's 90 percent completed. Then you come to price. Can't the seller compromise a little here?

The deal is mostly completed. The seller has invested a lot of time and is more likely to come down $5,000.

It's a start, and negotiations continue.

Make Sure the Sellers Know You Know Their Motivation

If the sellers know that you're aware of why they are selling, they will feel that they are in an inferior position. The sellers will be thinking something like, "This buyer knows we have to sell, so he or she will never come up to our price. But we do have to sell. So we may have to take less than we want."

Don't bully the sellers with this, but just have your agent mention that the buyer is aware that a job transfer is the reason the property is available and that is factored into the buyer's offer. That will make the sellers sit up and take notice. They may assume that every buyer will do likewise (particularly if the sellers haven't had other offers) and it may be a compelling reason to sign.

There are many other negotiating arguments and tactics that you can use. To check into these, I suggest you read my book, *Tips & Traps When Negotiating Real Estate,* McGraw-Hill, 1995.

Do I Have the Right Attitude?

Thus far we've been looking only at the seller. But if you want to get the right price, a lot depends on you. You must have the right attitude going into the deal to succeed.

The right attitude is more than just evaluating the property to come up with an appropriate price or knowing the market or the seller's motivation or even delivering the right arguments. The right attitude comes down to one thing: believing that you are more than just a consumer of real estate, believing that you are also an investor.

A consumer falls in love with a product and must have it. So the consumer buys it, regardless of cost. (If it costs too much, the consumer waits and saves up more money . . . or uses a credit card!)

The investor operates differently. If the price is too high or the terms are too onerous or something else is wrong, the investor passes. The investor isn't emotionally committed to the purchase. The investor can say, *"no!"*

You have to learn how to think like the investor. Sometimes negotiations go nowhere. Sometimes sellers simply won't budge. To get the property, you'll have to pay more than the right price, and that'll put you in jeopardy if you must sell early. That's the time to just say "no."

But that's hard to do, particularly if you've fallen in love with that darling breakfast nook off the kitchen. Or have a thing for the deep blue tile in the bathroom. When it comes time to say "No," your consumer instincts may kick in and goad you into paying more than you should just to get the property.

How do you hold back? How do you become more investor and less consumer?

The answer is having an alternative.

Do You Have an Alternative Home?

My suggestion is that you never simply make an offer on one home. Rather you find at least two, preferably three or four, that are equally appealing to you.

Yes, you can do this. In any given market there are hundreds, probably thousands of homes that will do. Most of the time our goal is to find just the right *one*. This time make the goal to find just the right *two* or *four* or more. If it helps, pretend that you're actually going to be buying more than one home. You're going to be buying three or four and pick out the best.

Try to get them to be equally attractive. Usually one will stand out, but try to find features in the others that compensate. In other words, try to make your consumer side be satisfied with any of the selections—one, two, three, or four. If you don't get number one, you'll be happy with number two, and so on.

If you can do this, you've put yourself in an amazingly strong position. You have an alternative.

When the negotiating gets tough and it comes down to, "Accept what the sellers are offering or lose the deal," you can smile at the agent (or the seller if you're presenting the offer) and say, "You lose. I've got other homes to buy." You can turn and walk away from a bad deal when you've got alternatives.

---

*N*ote

Sometimes walking away can be a strategic move. The sellers may have been convinced that you'd finally fold and buy the property. Walking away may shake them to their boots and they may hurriedly come back with a compromise offer you may want to consider. No, it doesn't happen all the time, but it does happen occasionally.

The alternative is what allows you to walk away gracefully. But what if you don't have an alternative home to make another offer on? That means that you must start the looking process all over—a daunting task. And you don't really know what you'll find, if anything at all.

Find an alternative home or two. It will make your negotiation far easier and more successful.

What Do I Do in a Tight Market?

Sometimes you'll be buying into a tight market where prices are going up and no matter how bad the condition of the property, no matter how motivated, you can't get the sellers to budge. They sense that if they hold out just a little bit longer, someone else will likely come along and offer more.

Tight markets do occur and as noted previously, they sometimes last a long time. And when they do, you can use them to your advantage.

If housing prices are going up by 5 percent a year for a few years, for example (as they have done in the past), and you believe they will continue to do so for a few more years, then don't hesitate to pay full market price.

After all, the price will go up whether the seller owns the property or you do. If you only need an increase of 5 percent to 8 percent to break even, you should be able to accomplish that in this market within a year or two, just because of price inflation.

This, in fact, was the way it was for a very long time in real estate during the 1960s, 1970s, and 1980s. There's no reason that a similar condition couldn't occur again by the end of the 1990s, although probably it will be far more short-lived.

When real estate everywhere is hot, jump in with both feet. The chances are very slim that you will get burned.

Can I Get the Seller to Accept My Offer?

We've looked at lots of different tactics and techniques that you can use to get the seller to accept your offer. Sometimes they will work with ease. Sometimes nothing will work.

What's important, however, is that you have faith in your offer. If you've calculated what you should pay for a property to be able to safely resell (see Chapter 12 if you're not sure), then don't go back and resharpen your pencil so that you can come up with a higher offer. That's usually an invitation to disaster.

Have confidence in your figures and stick to your guns. No, not every seller is going to be compliant and not every argument is going to work. But eventually, if you're persistent, you will find a seller who will sell the right house to you at the right price.

---

*C*hecklist for Negotiating with Sellers

- ❏ Have you figured the price "range" for the home?
- ❏ Do you know where in the range you should offer?
- ❏ Have you evaluated the home's condition?
- ❏ Have you evaluated the home's asking price?
- ❏ Have you evaluated the owner's motivation?
- ❏ Have you evaluated the market?
- ❏ Have you evaluated your competition?
- ❏ Have you insisted on a time limit for your offer?
- ❏ Are you getting the seller to invest time?
- ❏ Have you avoided the "pie analogy"?
- ❏ Are you working on the easy problems first?
- ❏ Are the sellers aware that you know their motivation?
- ❏ Do you have an alternative purchase in mind?

You want lots of checks here. The more checks, the better you've done your homework. Remember, knowing the right price to pay is only half the battle. The other half is getting the seller to accept it.

CHAPTER 14

Special Problems with Condos and Co-ops

Buying right and selling high with a condo or co-op can be a bit trickier than with a single-family home. There are considerations here that don't usually apply to a house. And some unique problems crop up and should be considered.

Should I Worry about Price Appreciation?

There's an old rule that has applied to many condo and co-op developments: they are the last to see price appreciation in good times, the first to have prices go down in a recession. Last up, first down has been the rule and there's enough truth in it to cause serious concern for any buyer.

First, however, what are we talking about? What is a condominium, town house, or co-op?

A condominium is shared ownership of a home. You own the airspace in your unit, but you share ownership with others for common areas such as walkways, pools, common land at front, rear and side, and so on. A town house is a type of condo where you also own the land beneath and the air above your unit. In a conventional condo, there might be other units above or below you.

A co-operative is a stock company. When you buy, you purchase stock in the corporation that allows you to use one of the units. Your title is to the stock, not to the property. For the purposes of this chapter, we'll be considering all three together, except where one or another is specified.

What Are the Advantages of Shared Ownership?

Shared ownership has many advantages. You don't have to worry about maintenance or repair of the common areas. That's handled by the HOA. Often, there are also many extras such as a pool, recreation center, tennis courts, and so on. These aren't found except in the most expensive single-family dwellings And then there is opportunity for social contact. Many times these organizations will have parties and gatherings for the members. Also, shared ownership can be ideal for owners who travel and who don't want the bother and fuss of taking care of a house.

Unfortunately, there are also drawbacks. Condo living can be like apartment living with far greater density than for single-family dwellings. There's more likelihood of noise from neighbors, there may be carports instead of garages, and there may be restrictions about what you can do at any given time (no loud late-night parties, for example). Furthermore, there's typically very little land. The most that a unit is likely to have is a small patch of ground in the back or perhaps a patio or deck.

Is It Less Desirable?

For many people the pluses outweigh the minuses. Unfortunately, however, shared housing generally has been viewed as less desirable than living in a single-family dwelling. There are several reasons for this. First, a condo or co-op in any given area usually sells for less than a comparable single-family dwelling. (The exceptions are resort and downtown urban areas.) This only stands to reason because the shared unit has far less land than the SFH.

The result of a lower cost, however, has meant that people who couldn't afford to buy a SFH have moved into the condo or co-op because they could afford shared housing. To those who care about such things, this has meant that they are less economically advantaged. In other words, the perception is that poorer people tend to live in condos and co-ops. (The actual facts do not necessarily bear this out.)

Furthermore, in many cases the construction of shared housing leaves something to be desired. During the 1970s and 1980s, for example, there were wave after wave of "conversions." A conversion is when a developer buys an apartment building and then converts it usually to condominium ownership. Too often only a cosmetic fix-up was done and the new owners took over an older, sometimes run-down building. This also puts a taint on shared ownership.

As a result, it was generally accepted that those who could afford a house, bought one. Those who couldn't, bought a condo or co-op. This was reflected in price appreciation, or the lack of it. Through the 1980s, condos and co-ops generally had much slower price appreciation. And when the market in general slowed, their prices froze. When the market accelerated, their prices rose only modestly. Until the real estate recession of the early 1990s. . . .

During the real estate recession, condos and co-ops did well or badly on a case-by-case basis. Those that were well located and well built and had a strong ratio of owners-to-tenants generally did better than the overall real estate market. Those that had a problem such as a poor location, a construction defect, or a high tenant ratio tended to fair worse.

Today, condos and co-ops present a viable option to the home hunter. However, it's important to be selective. Make the right choice and you could do as well as if you had bought an SFH. Choose poorly and you'll probably lose money even in a good market.

How Do I Tell Whether a Condo/Co-op Is Good or Bad?

Discriminating between the good developments and the not-so-good ones is not actually that hard, if you know what to look for. We'll consider several of the most important factors.

Tenant Population

This is probably the easiest problem to diagnose and also the most serious. Whether you believe it or not, it's a fact of life that an owner will tend to take better care of a property than a tenant. Having been a landlord for many years, I can testify to the truth of this statement. Even the best tenants feel that anything that goes wrong is someone else's problem and don't give it the care they would if something of theirs went wrong.

Furthermore, tenants in general (there are many exceptions) tend to be noisier than owners. It seems that owners are very concerned about the neighborhood and about protecting property values. Tenants, obviously, don't have such concerns.

As a result, tenants in condos and co-ops tend to be a drag on the property. Of course, almost all developments will have some tenants and a few are usually absorbed with no problems.

As the ratio of tenants-to-owners climbs, however, more problems (and complaints) tend to occur. When that ratio hits 25 percent (75 percent owners) or higher, it tends to impact on the value of the shared property. Too many tenants and the place becomes more like an apartment building than a condo.

Therefore, the first question I always ask is what is the tenant/owner ratio? If it's below 15 percent, I'll consider the property. Fifteen percent to 25 percent is marginal and more than 25 percent, for me, makes it unacceptable.

Besides, you have to ask yourself, why are so many owners renting out their units? Is it because they are investors instead of owner/occupiers (not a good sign)? Is it because they want to sell and can't? Is it because the development is in a better rental than sales market? Too many tenants and not enough owners has to be considered a warning indicator.

How do I find out the ratio?

Ask the agent. Ask the seller. Ask the homeowners association. Knock on a few doors and ask those who answer. You can be right up front. Say you're considering buying a unit and you're wondering if there are a lot of tenants in the building. If you happen to knock on the door of a tenant, you'll probably get a very straight answer. If it's an owner, you might take the answer with a grain of salt. (Remember, owners want more owners, not more tenants.)

Should I Check the Condition of the Property?

When buying a condo or co-op, the tendency is to be concerned only with the individual unit. After all, that is what you are basically purchasing. A lot of time is spent looking at the unit's walls and ceilings and the condition of the water heater and furnace.

Unfortunately, almost no time is spent examining the overall property. Yet, you are also buying, in common with others, all of the property, its buildings and amenities. What that means is that if anything is wrong with the rest of the property, you will have to pay your share to have it fixed. And if something major is wrong, a bond might be floated to pay the cost that would increase your monthly payments and would impact on your ability to resell later on.

So what do you check? Following is a list of potential physical problem areas for condos, town houses, and co-ops.

These are just a few of the items to check, but they should give an indication of the overall condition of the property. Don't hesitate to have your home inspector (who will check out the inside of your unit) conduct an inspection of the overall property. It should cost little more (if anything) and it could make a big difference in your decision to purchase.

*P*otential Physical Problem Areas to Check

Roof—If the property is more than ten years old, you should be concerned about the roof. Roof replacement is very costly, in the tens of thousands of dollars for a large building.

Pool—Most developments have one or more swimming pools. Are they cracked or in good condition? Is the equipment in need of repair?

Paint—If you have to paint your unit, you can probably do it in a few weekends and with a half dozen gallons of paint. If the entire development has to be painted, it can take months and can cost a small fortune.

Driveways—Are they in good shape or are they cracked? Cracked cement must be replaced, which usually is very costly. Cracked asphalt can be recoated and in this way, repairs can be delayed for many years.

Construction—Are there lots of cracks? Has the foundation shifted? Do doors bind when you try to close them? Do windows not meet properly? These are bad signs indicating poor construction.

Landscaping—It should be neat, trim, and lush. Anything less means that it may need special gardening to bring it back into shape, again a costly expense.

Should I Check Out the Homeowners Association?

Finally, the most common problems with shared ownership come from the associations set up to take care of them. If you discover a bad HOA, stay away from the development no matter how good the other areas may seem. A bad HOA is like the kiss of death.

What is a bad homeowners association? I've belonged to them and can assure you that I wished I hadn't.

Note

The fact that a building is in need of repair does not necessarily indicate a problem. A bad roof, for example, is going to happen eventually. What's important is that there is a reserve of money set aside to take care of it. If there is, then the repair isn't a problem, it's merely another task that the HOA should take care of. If you find what you think are problems, then go looking to see if the organization has already discovered the problem and is ready to deal with it. A problem dealt with is no problem at all.

First, let's consider a well-run HOA. Typically, this will have a board of directors who hires a manager (if the development is large enough) or an outside management company. Regular, orderly meetings are held. Reserve funds are set up and fully funded to handle expected and unexpected problems. (Adequate reserve funds are now required by some states.) The manager or management firm is available and capable of dealing with your questions as well as with the normal day-to-day problems that occur. There are no lawsuits, no angry owners ready to burst down the HOA's doors, no problems with the state about noncompliance with any laws. There's even a regularly published newsletter to keep you up-to-date on what's happening. In short, it's a well-run organization on top of everything.

Now let's consider a bad HOA. Here the board of directors may be feuding with one another and regular meetings are often canceled and rescheduled. At these meetings the board members argue vehemently with one another, their arguments punctuated by the loud complaints of owners in the audience. Sometimes things get out of hand with the yelling leading to fisticuffs—yes, I've seen this happen!

There may be reserve funds, but they often are tapped to pay for unexpected emergency expenses. (These types of unexpected events should have been anticipated.) When you call wanting to talk with someone, nobody seems to be in charge. Eventually, a board member may talk with you but may sound (and actually be) angry because you're a time distraction from something else. There's probably no newsletter and worst of all, the HOA may be the subject of one or more lawsuits from owners or the subject of a noncompliance problem with the state.

This may be a real can of worms. Living in the development might not be fun because of angry owners. And if the organization does not have enough insurance, you as an individual owner could be liable for damages resulting from a lost lawsuit. (In case you're wondering, the most common lawsuit involves a disgruntled homeowner who, typically, didn't get his or her way with the board and now is suing to achieve an aim. In a well-run organization, explanations are given and ruffled feathers soothed. In a badly run organization, ultimatums and tantrums are more common.)

In other words, the quality of the HOA is going to determine, in large part, the quality of life you enjoy in the shared ownership development. Bad HOAs will make your life miserable. And ultimately, what's miserable for you, will be noticeably miserable for the next buyer when you want to resell. A bad HOA will make reselling much more difficult.

How Do I Tell If the HOA Is Bad?

In most states before you buy, the HOA must release a statement of its condition to you. This should reveal whether there are any lawsuits pending and whether there are any compliance problems.

The HOA also must release a financial statement that will show how it spends the annual dues. It also should show the state of reserves, if any, what they are for, and when they are expected to be needed. This should jibe with your inspection of the property.

In addition, you should be provided with a set of the bylaws and the CC&Rs (Conditions, Covenants, and Restrictions) that govern the organization. You can check out these to see how elections are held, the composition of the board, and so forth. It's a good idea to have your real estate attorney also check out these materials.

If the HOA is unwilling or unable to release such information, I certainly would back off the deal.

Another good way of determining how well the HOA is running things is to get a history of dues. You'll be required to pay dues, usually monthly, to the HOA from which it will pay for expenses such as maintaining common areas and will set aside reserves.

Check the history. Has there been a steady, moderate progression of small increases over the years? If so, that's a good sign.

On the other hand, have dues been very low for a period of years, then suddenly shot up, then later been reduced only to shoot up even higher? This is a bad sign. It indicates lack of foresight in preparing for problems. Some HOAs will keep dues artificially low to placate members (who never want to pay any dues at all) by not funding reserves. Thus, when a roof needs to be replaced or the building repainted, there's no money to handle it. Suddenly, the dues have to be increased. Once the problem is paid for, they are artificially lowered until the next problem occurs. The pattern continues and is reflected in the dues history. Be wary of any HOA with spikes in dues. (Besides, the current dues might suddenly be raised and not only would you have to pay more, but any future buyer would be put off by the higher amount.)

If the HOA doesn't supply you with the information directly, ask your agent or the seller to obtain it. If your agent can't supply it to you, you have to ask yourself if it is because the organization is so badly run, or if it is because they have something to hide? (Most states require HOAs to provide financial information to would-be buyers.)

Is Shared Ownership for You?

Condos, town houses and co-ops offer alternative lifestyles that many find appealing. I personally have had it with working in the yard, mowing lawns, and trimming shrubs. I don't want to take care of a swimming pool or a spa. And I don't like the social isolation that often occurs in a neighborhood of single-family dwellings. On the other hand, I do like a park-like setting in which to live and I like the amenities such as rec center, pool, tennis court, and spa. And I like to have increased social contacts. Therefore, for me, a shared-ownership type of living is ideal.

However, just because it's the lifestyle of choice, doesn't mean I'm going to run out and buy the first town house or co-op that offers a good price. As we've seen in this chapter, you must be very selective when you buy if you want to have any hope of reselling later on to break even or show a profit.

Shared ownership is great, if you buy the right property. But it can be a real nightmare if you don't.

---

*C*hecklist for Condos and Co-ops

❏   Have you checked past price appreciation?

❏   Do you understand the type of shared ownership you're buying?

❏   Are you aware of the pros and cons?

❏   Do you know the tenant population ratio?

❏   Have you checked the property's condition?

❏   Have you checked out the HOA?

Shared ownership is not for everyone. But if you check it out carefully, you may find it's just perfect for you.

CHAPTER 15

Tax Planning When You Buy

Property is an enormous investment, and there are also enormous tax consequences when you buy property. For example, assuming that it's your principal residence, if you sell for a profit, you'll owe tax on your capital gain. On the other hand, if you sell for a loss, you probably can't take a tax deduction. (Limited deductions for loss now are being considered by Congress and may be in effect by the time you read this.)

Therefore, it can be enormously helpful to have some idea of what the tax consequences of home ownership are *before* you leap. Planning ahead is what investors do, and what you should do as well. In this chapter, we'll consider some things you might do before you buy and other things to consider while you own the property, long before you resell.

Before You Begin

It's important to understand that the tax laws of the United States are complex and to some extent arcane. They are filled with rules and details that can change what would, on the surface, appear simple and straightforward. Furthermore, the tax codes are in constant flux. The courts, Congress, and the

Internal Revenue Service (IRS) frequently change the rules or their interpretation of the rules. Before taking any action that has tax consequences, therefore, you are urged to consult with a competent tax specialist such as a certified public accountant (CPA) or a tax attorney. My purpose here is simply to provide an overview. I am not offering legal, tax, accounting, or other professional service.

How Should I Take Title?

There are many ways you can take title to property when you buy. For example, you can take title as tenants in common, as joint tenants (with right of survivorship), or you can hold title as community property (in some states) if you are married. You should check with an attorney to see what options and consequences are open to you.

One method, community property, or as it is known in some states, tenancy in entirety, has a provision in the tax code that can be extremely favorable under bad circumstances, namely the death of a spouse. If one spouse should die, the other then receives title to the property on a "stepped-up" basis. This has enormous implications with regard to capital gains. Let's see how.

When you sell property for a profit, you owe a tax on your capital gain. The capital gain is calculated in a very precise way. Put simply, it is the difference between what you paid for the property, plus any improvements, less some items and what you sell the property for, less the costs of the sale. For example, if you buy a home for $100,000 and then sell it later on for $200,000, you're going to have to pay tax on the gain.

That tax can be fairly stiff. As of this writing, it is at a maximum of 28 percent. If your capital gain were $100,000, you could end up owing $28,000 in taxes. That's a hefty amount to give to Uncle Sam, and there would very likely also be state taxes to pay.

As we'll see, payment of this tax can be deferred, *if* you roll over the property. However, the tax can be avoided entirely if you take title as community property and one spouse dies. The surviving spouse gets a stepped-up basis, which means that the property is reevaluated at the time of death and its value at that time is the new basis. For example, the original basis may have been $100,000 from when the property was purchased. But at the time of the spouse's death, the property's value was actually $200,000. That becomes the new basis and now, if the remaining spouse sells before it appreciates further, there is no tax to pay.

Although few of us contemplate dying soon, taking title in the right way is an important consideration *before* we buy. As noted, it is well worth the cost of a few minutes of an estate attorney's time to explain the rules, the options, and the consequences to get it right.

How Can I Defer the Tax When I Sell?

"Deferring" means putting off until tomorrow what you would otherwise owe today. In terms of the sale of real estate, it means that instead of paying the tax on the capital gain you may owe when you sell, you put it off or "defer" to the future. It doesn't mean it's forgiven, overlooked, or exempted. You still owe it, just not now.

If you live in the home you buy and it's your principal residence (your main home, should you have more than one), and you sell it and replace it with another principal residence of equal or greater value within two years, you don't have to worry about deferring the gain on the sale. The government doesn't give you an option, you must defer it.

What happens is that the gain is rolled over into the new house, and when you go to resell that house, you'll owe the gain you deferred from the *first* house, unless you roll it over again. There's no limitation to the number of times you can roll over the gain, provided you meet the ground rules. These include:

- It must be your principal residence (It can be a house, condo, co-op, one-half of a duplex, a houseboat, or, in some cases, even a recreational vehicle [RV]!).

- You can roll over a principal residence only once every two years. If you sell and buy and resell again in a shorter time period, then you will owe capital-gains tax (if there was a gain) on one of the sales.

- To get the full deferral, the new property must be of the same or greater value as the old property. If it's of lesser value, then only a portion of the gain may be deferred.

- You must replace the sold property within four years, two years either before or after the sale. If it's a new construction, you must actually occupy the new home within two years.

- Special rules may apply if you're in the armed services or are forced to sell sooner than two years because of a job change. Check with your accountant or tax attorney.

- This rule is not optional. If you qualify, you must take it.

How Can I Get in Trouble with the Rollover?

It's easy. Just rent out your home for a time.

When we buy, as noted in the first and second chapters, almost all of us contemplate living in the home forever. However, circumstances change. We may need to move and not be able to sell. Therefore, we rent out the property. Or we may have a chance to move up to a bigger and better home and decide to keep the original property as a rental.

Once we no longer live in the home, it stops being our principal residence. (Wherever else we live now gets that title.) If we don't rent it out, it may become a second home. If we rent it out, we've converted it to rental property.

Now we may not be able to utilize the rollover. It's important to understand that the rollover applies only to our principal residence, and we can have only one at a time. It does not apply simply to residential property. It does not apply to our second home (not our principal residence) and definitely does not apply to rental property.

Thus, by converting our principal residence to rental property, we may lose one of the best benefits the tax laws allow.

Can't I Convert It Back?

The rules tend to be in a gray area. Generally speaking, however, if you rent out your home for two years, even if you take depreciation during that period, you still can claim it as your principal residence when you sell. More than two years and you'd probably have a fight on your hands with the IRS.

On the other hand, if you rent it out for more than two years, and then move back in to reestablish it as your principal residence, once again you probably could claim the rollover. It would be a matter of deciding on an individual basis and the issues would be how long it was rented out, how long you lived in it originally, and how long you occupied it when you moved back.

Thus, some planning is in order here. Unless you want to give up a lot of your profit in taxes, you'd better plan ahead about when you're going to be living in the property and when you are not.

As noted, if you never leave, you've probably got no problem. But if you do decide to rent it out, keep the rollover rule in mind. Rent it out for too long and it becomes rental property. Rent it out for a shorter period of time and you can probably safely use the rollover rules.

It's certainly something to keep track of. Be sure to check with your tax adviser to see how the rule plays out for your own circumstances.

Aren't There Advantages to Renting Out Real Estate?

What about renting out my home? Doesn't that offer some tax pluses?

Yes, there are some pluses, but not nearly so many as there used to be. Prior to 1986 you could deduct any loss on the ownership of real estate from your ordinary income. In other words, if you owned a rental property and it showed a $5,000 loss, that was a deduction you could take on your income taxes.

Note

Rental real estate often shows an annual loss, on paper, mainly because of depreciation. You subtract all your actual expenses from your rental income (including costs of going to visit the property, advertising, a portion of telephone expenses, and so on) and then, in addition, you subtract a sum for depreciation, which only appears on paper. This usually pushes most rental properties into the red.

With the Tax Reform Act of 1986, however, the government decreed that all rental real estate was automatically a passive investment. That meant that while the loss on one property could be deducted from the gain on another, the loss could not be deducted from your ordinary income.

This killed the real estate write-off for big players. For small investors, however, it still may be alive. There was a special allowance of up to a $25,000 deduction for people making less than $150,000 a year. This remains in effect as of this writing, but it involves some complicated rules. Check with your tax adviser.

If you're a small investor, therefore, you still may be able to write off a substantial portion of your "loss" if you rent out your home. Thus, converting to a rental property, at least for a few years, may yet be an option you want to consider.

What Is the $125,000 Once-in-a-Lifetime Exclusion?

Can I exclude a portion of my gain if I'm a senior citizen?

Probably. The final issue we'll deal with is the $125,000 exclusion that's been on the tax books for some time.

Basically, this rule was set up to allow older Americans (those age 55 and more) to sell an expensive home and buy into a less-expensive home. Chances are over the years they had rolled over many homes so that when the children finally left and it came time to sell and downsize, they would owe a huge capital gains tax.

Provided that certain conditions were met, under this rule the senior citizen could take a $125,000 exclusion. That meant that the first $125,000 of gain simply vanished. The government pretended it didn't exist and no tax was owed on it.

Furthermore, this $125,000 exclusion could be combined with the rollover so that the senior citizen then could roll over the remaining gain into a smaller home. The actual calculation is fairly complicated, but in a simplified form, if you sold a home for $300,000 that had a basis of $100,000, there would be a gain of $200,000. Now, however, the first $125,000 would be excluded by the once-in-a-lifetime rule. That meant that the $200,000 gain was reduced to $75,000. And, if the taxpayer now rolled over into a home costing at least $175,000, that $75,000 of gain could continue to be deferred. If the house cost less, probably a portion of the gain could be deferred. The rule allows senior citizens to get out and downsize.

But there are some very strict provisions for getting the benefit here and those require careful planning. They include the following:

- It must be your principal residence (it can be a house, condo, co-op, one-half of a duplex, a houseboat, or, in some cases, even a recreational vehicle [RV]!).

- At least one spouse must be 55 on the day of the sale.

- It is not mandatory. You have to elect to take it. But if you do, you can do it only once in a lifetime.

- If one spouse elects to take the exclusion, he or she also takes it for the other spouse. The second spouse cannot take it again at a later time.

- You must have lived in the home as a principal residence for the previous three out of five years.

A number of other conditions exist along with some fairly complex interpretations. If you are contemplating going for this exclusion, be sure to see your tax adviser first.

What If I Rent Out the Property?

Once again, this is where planning is vital. You may rent out the property and still claim the exclusion. But you cannot rent it out for more than two years in the five-year period prior to making the claim. If you rent it out for even one day over the two-year period, you lose your right to make the claim.

For this reason, if you are nearing the age of 55 and are planning to take this once-in-a-lifetime exclusion, you would be wise to consider very carefully any conversion of the home to rental property. If you do convert it, watch the dates closely. Be sure that you don't rent it for more than two years.

Should I Wait to Take the Exclusion?

This is always a consideration. Because you can only take it once in a lifetime, should you take it now . . . or save it for a future property?

*N*ote

Unlike with the two-year rule for the rollover, there is no gray area here. The rule is quite specific: it must be your principal residence for three out of the previous five years.

A lot depends on the amount of your gain. Is it the full $125,000? If it's less, you can't save the unused portion for later use.

Do you plan to buy a less-expensive home? If not, the rollover probably will do just as well for you as the exclusion, which you can save.

These and other questions are surely something you will want to consider carefully before deciding whether or not to take the once-in-a-lifetime $125,000 exclusion. They are also the reasons you will want to confer with your tax adviser over the issues.

There may be one further consideration and that is what the government will do in the future. Many of us feel that the government giveth and the government taketh away. As of this writing, the once-in-a-lifetime $125,000 exclusion is in effect. But who knows what will happen tomorrow? The government, intent on reducing the federal budget and finding new ways of increasing income, could, with a couple of swipes of a pen, remove the exclusion. Some people feel that this is a good reason for taking it as soon as you can.

On the other hand, both major political parties have promised at one time or another to dramatically increase the size of the exclusion or to simply excuse any gain from the sale of a principal residence up to a huge amount, as much as half a million dollars. If you believe that tax relief in this form is on its way, then you may want to wait before selling your property and taking the exclusion.

What should be clear is that from a tax perspective, it's important to plan ahead both at the time you buy and during your tenure of ownership. Make a mistake and it could prove very costly. Plan well and it could save lots of tax dollars.

---

*C*hecklist for Tax Planning

❑   Have you discussed how to take title with your attorney?

❑   Are you aware of the "rollover" rules?

❑   Are you aware of the "conversion" problems?

❑   Are you aware of the "$125,000 exclusion"?

❑   Have you checked with a tax specialist about getting the exclusion?

Planning for the future can save you loads of taxes. You should have checked all of the above. If not, go back and reread the chapter.

How Long Will It Take You to Resell?

Many intangible issues are involved when buying a home, not the least of which is how long will it take and how hard will it be to resell? If you're experienced in real estate, you probably already have a feel for this. But if you are not, this can be perplexing.

In this Appendix we're going to look at reselling your home sometime in the (distant) future. Here's what you'll probably go through.

One Agent or Many?

Should you work with just one agent or many? For those relatively new to selling real estate, this can be somewhat confusing.

A variety of different types of listings are available. These include the following:

Exclusive right to sell—one agent only who gets a commission even if you find the buyer and sell the property!

Exclusive agency—one agent only who only gets a commission if the agent comes up with a buyer. You don't pay if you find the buyer.

Open listing—lots of agents. You'll pay whomever comes up with a buyer. You don't pay if you find the buyer.

Obviously, most agents want the first arrangement, the exclusive right to sell. It ties you up and guarantees them a commission no matter what, if the property sells. On the other hand, many sellers want the open listing. It ties you up the least and you only have to pay a commission if one of many agents actually brings in a buyer.

Which do I recommend? Surprising to some, the exclusive right to sell, always.

Why? It's simple. The reason you want an agent in the first place is to find a buyer for you. This means that you want an agent who will spend time, money, and effort on your property. But will any agent do that if he or she knows that the place can be sold out from under him or her if you find a buyer, or if another agent finds a buyer? Would *you* spend time, effort, and money on such a chancy proposition?

Only by guaranteeing the agent a commission on a sale can you hope to gain that agent's full cooperation in finding a buyer. Of course, in return you can expect a lot from that agent, as we'll see next.

By the way, don't worry about not having many agents working on your property in an exclusive right-to-sell listing. Once given to one agent, that person can in turn (and usually does) cobroke with all the other agents in the area. Yes, you only owe a commission to one agent. But that one agent can split that commission with any number of other agents.

*H*int

Always insist that the agent list your property on the local multiple listing service, which means cobroking with the vast majority of other agents in the area. It's a service that your agent should provide.

Which Agent Should You Pick?

Knowing you're going to pick an agent, the question now becomes, which one?

Unfortunately, too often the answer is Uncle Freddy, who happens to be in real estate, isn't doing particularly well right now, and needs some help. Wrong reason to list!

Remember, selling a property is business, your business. If you take longer to sell, it's more money out of your pocket in monthly mortgage payments as well as in taxes, insurance, and whatever other costs you may have running with the property. If Uncle Freddy lists the property for six months and never finds a buyer, it's a big money loss for you. Therefore, you want to pick your agent carefully.

Should you choose an independent or one who works for one of the big franchise companies such as RE/MAX or Century 21?

The franchise companies offer certain advantages to their agents such as relocation services (someone sells their home in one part of the country and then comes to another part and uses the same franchise agency), massive advertising, standardized procedures and documents, and a presumably responsible party to turn to in case something goes wrong. All of these are worth considering. All agents, however, are licensed everywhere in the country, and most independents also provide good service and are members of a multiple-listing board just like the franchises.

In my opinion, the real issue is not the company but the agent. What you want is someone who will actively work on selling your property and come up with a buyer. If that person happens to be an independent or working for a franchise, that is irrelevant. The person himself or herself is the most important consideration. What do you look for in a good agent?

You obviously want someone who is totally honest, who is personable, and who is available (which means it's usually best to avoid the many part-time agents who are in business across the country). But, most important to finding a buyer, you want an agent who is well known in the industry and who is extremely active among other agents.

Remember, at any given time, 90 to 95 percent of all buyers in an area are working with agents. What you want your particular agent to do is to "talk up" your property so that other agents will learn about it.

Yes, having your property listed in the multiple-listing book is important. But yours could be one of thousands. What's needed is for your agent to get on the telephone and begin calling other agents in different offices and telling them about this great property that he or she has listed. Your agent needs to stand up at real estate board meetings and promote your property and get other agents excited about it.

How do you recognize an agent who is active like this?

You can ask around. Other agents know who's tops in their field and will often let it slip. Or you can simply ask to see the broker in an office and then ask which agent sold the most properties in the past year. The broker probably will give you a straight answer. Or you can simply ask the one you're talking to, "How many properties, exactly, have you sold in the past six months?" An answer of at least one a month shows an active agent.

R**ule**

Remember 80/20—80 percent of the property is sold by 20 percent of the agents.

How Long Should You List?

Most agents I know, particularly the good ones, want long listings. They would like listings of six months, sometimes nine months or even a year. Their reasoning is understandable. In the uncertain real estate markets in most parts of the country over the past few years, it's simply impossible to know how long it will take to sell. They don't want to spend a lot of time, money, and energy on a property, only to lose the listing to someone else before it sells.

On the other hand, long listings, in my opinion, are bad for sellers. The reason is simply that if you give a long listing and the agent turns out to be a turkey (doesn't work hard for you), it's a long time before you can switch. (You can't cancel a listing once given, only the agent can.)

I suggest a listing of three months. I also suggest that you make it perfectly clear that if the agent does a good job and the house just doesn't happen to sell, you'll certainly relist for another three months and again, if necessary.

A good agent will recognize that you're concerned about getting action on your property and although he or she may still push for a longer listing, the agent probably will agree to the three-month period. This is particularly the case if you've priced your property to sell. (Reread Chapter 12 if you're not sure about this.) A good agent will recognize that a well-priced property should sell quickly and shouldn't hesitate about accepting a shorter-term listing.

On the other hand, if your agent absolutely refuses to accept a three-month listing, you have to ask yourself why? Is it because the agent has no confidence about selling the property quickly? And if that's the case, do you want to use that kind of agent?

When Should You Try a New Agent?

Which brings us, finally, to the matter of switching agents. If you try an agent for three months and there's little action, of course consider switching. But how do you really know if your agent has been active? Maybe it's just that the market's been slow.

There are a number of telltale signs. For example, have you had many offers? If you've had offers that were reasonably good, but just not quite up to what you want and you've turned them down, you know your property's getting a lot of attention.

Similarly, have there been a lot of agents streaming through scouting your property for their buyers? Don't be fooled by the caravans that agents conduct when you first list. Yes, these are important as everyone in the agent's office comes by to see your property on caravan day. But you want lots of agents coming by continually on a regular basis. This means that your agent has been talking up your property to others. (If you're not there, you can check the activity by the cards left behind. Every time an agent comes by, he or she normally leaves a business card. More than one card from the same agent usually means he or she came by once to check out the property and then brought buyers by a second time.)

Have you seen your property advertised in the newspaper? Has the agent held an open house? (Open houses don't usually help you directly, for statistics indicate that buyers who stop by open houses almost never buy that house. But it does suggest that your agent is making an effort to be active in the market-place.)

On the other hand, what if there's no activity? What if after a month or so you find that your agent is one of those who lists and leaves? Your choices are not good. About all you can do is to ask the agent for your listing back.

Most agents are quite sensitive to public opinion. Even if they refuse to release your listing, asking for it back may spur them on to greater efforts. If they refuse and you still want to get your listing back, you can threaten to take legal action, although they as well as you should realize that this is an unlikely option. Almost all listings simply say that the agents will make a best effort at selling the property and unless you've specified something such as advertising every weekend—something most agents will refuse to accept in a listing—it's hard to prove that they haven't made a best effort.

If they're a member of a local real estate board, you can complain to the board. Keep in mind, however, that the board is composed of other agents and they're used to hearing sellers complain that their properties haven't sold as fast as they want.

You should have some specific examples to back up your complaint. The board may talk to your agent and work out some type of a compromise by which the agent does release your listing early. This might be the case particularly if there's been no action and there doesn't seem to be much chance of the property selling soon.

Finally, if all else fails, you can simply wait until the listing runs out, hoping that another agent will discover your property and sell it to a buyer. After all, chances are you won't find out that your agent is a turkey for a month or two and by then you've only got a few weeks left on your listing. (You did only sign up for a three-month listing, didn't you?)

Knowing what you're up against when it comes time to sell can help you more clearly calculate what you need to spend (in terms of time and money) when you buy.

Will You Be Able to Resell by Yourself?

In Chapter 12, we discussed reselling as a consideration when buying. One of the concerns was reducing your purchase price so that you could resell almost immediately, if need be. The more you cut what you can pay, however, the less likely you are to get a deal. In this chapter we're going to consider how to cut your resale costs so you can afford to offer more when you buy. We're going to look into what's involved with selling FSBO (For Sale By Owner).

How Do You Find Potential Buyers?

When people are looking for homes (other than brand-new homes), they usually consult first with a real estate agent. After all, agents typically have the vast majority of properties in the area listed. The agent can easily provide them with a list of homes that have sold recently, then buyers can quickly see what market values are. And the agent happily drives them to the different properties that are available.

You have almost none of these options. (You can easily get a list of recent sales from a broker; most are very willing to help you out when you sell FSBO, anticipating that at some point you'll give up and, hopefully, list with them.) Therefore, you have to be creative in your efforts to get buyers to come by and look at your property. There are at least six different methods that you can employ to locate buyers and we'll consider each here.

1. Advertising

You will need to advertise your property. However, advertising is expensive. A three-inch advertisement in a local newspaper can cost several hundred dollars just for a weekend run. If you had to put the ad in for a month or more, you could quickly spend a lot of the money you anticipated saving by not listing with an agent. (If you think agent's fees are high, here's clear evidence of one of their major expenses.)

On the other hand, you really don't need a big ad. You have two magic words that will draw buyers to your ad like a cat to fish—"By Owner." Remember, buyers are price-conscious and are always looking for a bargain. When they see a FSBO ad, their antennae go up. From their perspective, you're a potential opportunity, one that their agents haven't told them about.

What this means to you is that instead of a three-inch ad, you only need a three-line ad. Always include the words, "By Owner." Then add in some of the essentials—the size of the house, the general location (so buyers will know what area of town you're in), the price (if possible emphasizing that it's below market), and your telephone number.

Your ad doesn't have to be clever or cute. It doesn't need to explain that you have two fireplaces and a spa. All it needs to get across is the idea of "Bargain!" and buyers will come running.

2. Word of Mouth

In addition to paid advertising, you can spread the word by talking up your property to everyone you meet. Of course, this includes your relatives and immediate friends, but it also means everyone else. You go to a barber or a hair stylist to have your hair cut; while you're sitting in the chair, describe this wonderful bargain you have for sale. Your stylist or barber will hear and may pass on the word. Others in the shop may hear and even if they are not interested themselves, they may tell their friends. You never know who's looking for a house. Or who knows someone who's looking?

You may attend business meetings, go to social events, even just take your children to soccer or baseball practice. Talk up the FSBO you have for sale, emphasizing the bargain you're offering. Mention that you have a house for sale below market price and I guarantee ears will prick up. Everyone's looking for a bargain. And word of a housing bargain spreads quickly.

Don't discount your ability to spread the word by talking up your property. Your probably see far more people in a week than you imagine and they see many more. No, you wouldn't want to attempt a sale *only* by spreading the word yourself. But, as one of many avenues, it is excellent.

3. Flyers

Real estate professionals use these all the time. Haven't you passed by a house with a "For Sale" sign on it that also carried a little box saying, "Take One." Inside was a flyer giving the price of the home, a brief description, the advantages of its location and showing a photo. If it works for the pros, it will work for you.

Putting together a flyer is easy. You can use any computer with a word processor and a printer to do the typesetting. (If you don't own a good one, they are readily and inexpensively available at copying stores such as Kinko's.) You can take a photograph with your 35mm camera and have it blown up at a camera store. Then the photograph can be duplicated on the same sheet as your description using a copying machine at the same store. (Ask the attendant to help out if you're not sure how it's done.)

Here's a list of items to include on your flyer:

---

*F*lyer Information

- Address
- Price
- Seller's name
- Seller's telephone number
- Lot size
- Age of house
- Shopping

- Nearby schools
- Size of house (bedrooms, baths, family/dining rooms)
- Size of garage
- Air-conditioned
- Pool
- Special features

In short, you can easily put together a flyer. Then you can build or buy a small box to attach to your sign (which will be discussed in the next section) and fill it with your flyers.

In addition, once you have your flyer ready, you should distribute it wherever you can. Nearly all supermarkets and large pharmacies as well as many other stores have bulletin boards. Attach your flyer to these (or condense it into a small 3×5″ card if necessary). One bold person I know actually took flyers into local real estate offices! She told the agents that she would pay them half a commission (to be discussed shortly) if they brought in buyers.

4. Put Up a Sign

Real estate pros know that a sign is one of the most important means of selling a property. Yet, many people who try to sell

FSBO are hesitant about putting up a sign and then when they do, use a $1.35 sign they bought at their local hardware store.

A sign lets people in your neighborhood know that your house is for sale, and one of them may want to buy it. A sign lets those who are driving by know you've got a home for sale and if you've got any traffic at all on your street, this can amount to an enormous number of people. And a sign directs people who have called on your ad or flyer to your house. When they call you can say, "My house is on Walnut Street. Just turn right and look for the sign."

Because a sign is so important, you should spend a little time and money on it. Get a professional to create a sign for you. Those in the field usually will create a sign for under $50. The sign doesn't have to say much, particularly if you have a flyer box underneath. It should just say:

For Sale
by Owner
Telephone Number

This provides the essential information. If there's some special attraction such as the number of bedrooms or a pool that you want to feature, by all means put it on the sign. But, as noted, the flyer should cover most items.

Place the sign where it is most visible on your lot. Some areas have restrictions on signs that require that you use a wood post of a special design instead of just a metal stake. Check with your homeowners association and planning department to find out.

5. Try Local Housing Offices

Another alternative is to contact large local companies. Many of these have housing offices that help when employees are transferred into and out of the area. Sometimes people in these offices will work with you.

Just call up or drop by and mention that you have a house for sale. Bring in a flyer and, if they're willing, leave a stack with them to pass out.

6. Try Electronic Media

This is a totally new method of finding buyers, one that you as a FSBO seller should give close consideration. Today, all local cable stations must provide a public-access channel. The trouble is, there's very little broadcasting available for that channel. In addition, many local stations offer paid broadcasting for very small businesses on one or more of their channels.

So, if you own or can borrow a camcorder, put together a short 30-second or one-minute video of your home. Show it from the front and back, walk through a couple of rooms that have nice features, such as the family room with the fireplace and the kitchen. All the time, talk about price, the discount you're offering, and any special terms you may be offering. And then try to get it on your local cable channels.

In some areas, because you're selling a product—your house—there will be resistance. If that's the case, redesign your commercial into an infomercial. Make it a five-minute piece describing how any homeowner can sell a property on his or her own. Of course, use your house as an example. If the professionals can sell hair paint and body stretchers, why can't you sell your house?

You also may want to consider going online. If there is a local Web page in your area that handles items for sale, use it. If there are local bulletin boards, post your house. An electronic advertisement may find a real buyer just as quickly and easily (and far less expensively) as a newspaper ad.

Answering Telephone Calls and Showing

When you list, an agent fields all the telephone calls and then screens potential buyers before bringing them by. When you sell by owner, you take on those chores. And you can handle them well, provided you're prepared.

But most important, be aware that you must be available at all times. Buyers are fickle by nature. They figure that they're the ones spending the money, so they should not be inconvenienced. If they want to see your house at 9 AM on Sunday morning, your one day a week to sleep in, you'd better be prepared to show it. If they call at 11 PM because they just found your advertisement and are excited about your property, be excited, too, even if you went to bed an hour earlier. When you sell FSBO (or even with an agent), you have to put yourself out and make yourself available. Of one thing you can be sure, no buyers are going to put themselves out to find you.

When someone calls, it's important that you answer in a business-like fashion and are ready to describe all the details of your property. It's also important that you are home to answer the telephone as much as possible.

If you're not home, you can use "call forwarding," which is available from most telephone companies, to get your call wherever you are. It's important to use this service because a potential buyer may call only once.

Finally, if you simply can't answer the telephone, be sure to have an answering machine connected. Leave a friendly message that assures the caller that the house is still for sale, you're just out for a short time, and you'll return the call right away.

Beware of having anyone who happens to be at home answer the telephone. In particular, try to avoid having children or teenagers answer. It could turn off a buyer and it's oh so easy to just hang up. Instead, designate a certain person to answer the telephone. If possible, have a dedicated telephone line just for potential buyers. (It costs only a few bucks to set up and you won't be spending a lot of money on outgoing calls.)

Is Security a Problem?

One of the big concerns when selling by owner is security. How do you know who you're inviting into your house? The person could be a buyer. Or a mugger, rapist, or thief.

The only honest answer is that you don't know. One of the important services that an agent performs is to screen buyers and then to accompany them when they look at a house. But, in truth, even agents don't always know with whom they're dealing.

There are some things you can do to help protect yourself. It's important to remember that there's no way to be completely safe.

I always emphasize that someone selling FSBO should avoid showing the house unless it's by appointment. First, have the person call. Talk to them on the telephone for awhile. They'll ask you lots of questions and you can ask a few in turn. Where do they currently live? What's their name? What's their telephone number? If they have a local address and telephone number (which you can confirm by calling the telephone company or looking up in the telephone book), at least you know they have a minimal presence in the community. No, it certainly doesn't guarantee that they don't have devious motives, but it's a start.

I also suggest that FSBO owners not show the property alone, particularly if they are women. Always have a friend or relative with you. Potential buyers won't think twice about it, but someone who has ill intents might reconsider.

Finally, if security is a real concern for you, then don't try selling FSBO. Instead, list with an agent. Again, there's no guarantee, but it is a lot safer.

How Do You Get Buyers to Commit?

All it takes is getting the buyer to sign on the dotted line. But how do you get to that step?

Agents will tell you it's salesmanship. I'm telling you that anyone, yourself included, can do it. After all, it's the product, your house, that ultimately has to sell itself. If the price is right, the house will sell. The key is getting out of the way.

When potential buyers come by, let them browse and think of the house as their own. (Of course, move any valuables out long before you begin showing the place—you can't be too careful.) Don't press buyers too closely with information and facts and don't expect instantaneous commitment on their part.

What you want potential buyers to do is to call back and come back. (That's why you should have a guest book in which all visitors sign in and give their telephone number so you can call them back later.)

---

int

You can exclude potential buyers whom you've already shown the property to when you list later on, even in an exclusive right-to-sell listing. If they come back, then you don't have to pay a commission. But you need their names and telephone numbers to do it.

It's rare that a potential buyer will commit on a first visit. But by the time that buyer comes back two or three times, you know that you've got a solid bite. Now you can stop talking about the benefits of the house and start talking financing.

Yes, as a FSBO seller you're going to need to help your buyer get financing, or at least help find a mortgage broker or other lender who can get it for the seller. You're also going to need to know enough about financing to know whether or not they'll qualify for a mortgage on your property. For help in this area, I suggest you look into my book, *Tips and Traps When Mortgage Hunting,* published by McGraw-Hill (1992).

Finally, at some point, the buyers are going to suggest or sometimes come right out and state that they want to buy your house. "Fine," you'll say. But now what? How do you document their commitment?

How Do You Handle the Paperwork?

My suggestion is that unless you're very familiar with real estate and have completed a lot of deals, you don't perform the paperwork yourself. Real estate documentation has become so complex in recent years that even some real estate agents are having trouble with it. Today a sales agreement may reach as many as ten pages in length and contain all types of required clauses that you may have never heard about. Thus, if you're a novice in the field and sell FSBO, the one area where you absolutely need professional help is with the documents.

Where do you get such help? There are two sources. In some areas real estate agents often will help do the paperwork for you for a fee. Sometimes that fee is a set amount, say $500. Other times it's a percentage of the sales price, maybe ½ percent to 3 percent. (For 3 percent, the agent should do a lot more work as well.) Check around with different agents to see if this is an option for you.

In many areas of the country (but not the Western states), real estate attorneys will handle the documentation. Often these people have set fees that may be around $1,000. They draw up the documents and offer you minimal, but essential, legal advice.

Thus, when you have buyers who are ready, willing, and able to purchase, I suggest you walk over to your professional and let the professional put the documentation together. Your chances of getting a solid deal without complications are much enhanced by doing this.

Should You Work with an Agent?

When you are trying to sell your home by owner, you need all the help you can get. And if you can get some professional help, you'd be crazy not to take it. Of course, you should only pay for what you get.

I always suggest that if an agent comes by saying something such as, "I have a probable buyer for your home. Will you let me show it and pay a commission?", you reply, "Certainly, I'll pay you a buying agent's commission of 3 percent" (or whatever half of the average rate in your area happens to be). Most agents with a legitimate buyer won't hesitate to move forward with this offer . . . and it's to your advantage. You end up paying only half a commission and you get a quicker sale.

Yes, you can sell by owner. But it's not free of work. What you essentially do when you sell FSBO is to perform the work the agent normally does and, as a consequence, keep at least part of the commission and perhaps get a faster sale. For more detailed information on this subject, look into *The For Sale By Owner Kit*, published by Dearborn Financial Publishing, Inc., 1995.

No, presumably you're not going to sell tomorrow. But if you had to, at least now you have some idea of what you're up against if you try to sell by owner. If it's not for you, then increase the amount of resale costs and reduce the amount you can afford to pay for the property. On the other hand, if reselling FSBO is really an option, you can afford to pay more when you buy.

INDEX